Zenobia

Zenobia

between Reality and Legend

YASMINE ZAHRAN

STACEY
INTERNATIONAL

Zenobia

First published by Archaeopress in 2003

This revised edition published by Stacey International in 2010 with a new preface.

Stacey International
128 Kensington Church Street
London W8 4BH
Telephone: +44 (0)20 7221 7166
Fax: +44 (0)20 7792 9288
Email: info@stacey-international.co.uk
www.stacey-international.co.uk

ISBN-978 1 90676838 6

Printed and bound in Great Britain by
CPI Antony Rowe, Chippenham, Wiltshire

CIP Data: A catalogue for this book is
available from the British Library

Fig. 1

Claudi Auguste, tu nos a Zenobia . . . libera!

Claudius Augustus, set us free from Zenobia!

The Roman Senate's plea to the Emperor Claudius, AD 268
(Historia Augusta, Claud., 4,4)

BOOKS BY THE SAME AUTHOR

Septimius Severus
Philip the Arab
Ghassan Resurrected
The Lakhmids of Hira
Echoes of History (Arabic)

Novels:
A Beggar at Damascus Gate
Al-Lahn El-Awal (Arabic)
Batin al-Hawa (Arabic)

Contents

LIST OF ILLUSTRATIONS

Plate section 3 (between pages 144 and 145)

Preface

This is a fascinating book and a highly rewarding read which is rich in history, character and insights. It combines Yasmine Zahran's skills as an accomplished historian of the Eastern Roman period and a talented novelist. Its most remarkable characteristic is the power of its multi-layered narrative: the author constructs the story of *Zenobia* as a Greek tragedy, with the various historians and their contradictory discourses as an unruly chorus. Like modern spin doctors, with their different ideological bent, each historian picks up the story from the other, and without examining its truthfulness, repeats, alters or embellishes it according to his purpose. The juxtaposition of narrative and history and their continual interaction, in which each seeks to authenticate its version, provides the book with depth, scope and vitality. It posits the creative narrative, and particularly the voice of the woman, which Zahran mastered in her novels (she has three novels to her name: one in English, *A Beggar at Damascus Gate*, and two in Arabic, *Al-Lahn al-Awwal* and *Batin al-Hawa'*) against the official discourse of the male historian. The result is the captivating story of Zenobia, which enables us to understand both the predicament of Arab women, and the long history of Orientalism; of the contending discourses of the West and the Orient.

While reading this book, I was often reminded of what the creative insight of Shakespeare did to the story of

Cleopatra in his *Anthony and Cleopatra*. Although it is well-established that Shakespeare draws the material of his Roman plays from Plutarch, the discrepancy between the two accounts of Cleopatra could not be greater. The Cleopatra that emerges from Plutarch's historical discourse of officialdom could not seduce a simple Roman, let alone an experienced military leader and sophisticated politician who saw the world and risked it all for her.

Shakespeare understood that, unlike the creative writer, the historian is no expert in the human psyche or the plausibility of the characters involved in the events he records. This is the business of the dramatist, hence the Cleopatra that emerges from the Shakespearian tragedy is much more humane and plausible a character than that portrayed by Plutarch. Plutarch's account is not only misogynist, but often racist and implausible. Shakespeare understood that in order to deserve the attention of Anthony, let alone his heart and mind, the real Cleopatra must be different from the one portrayed by Plutarch. Indeed, Shakespeare's creative insight enabled him to discern the real Cleopatra through the tissue of lies and prejudices woven by the official historian. The interesting thing, or rather the irony of history, is that subsequent historians proved that the real Cleopatra was much closer to the one discerned by Shakespeare, through the power of his dramatic imagination, and without any historical research, than to that of Plutarch who must have done his historical research.

Unlike Shakespeare, who was not interested in history but, rather, in the drama of humanity and the affairs of the heart, Zahran combines both in doing for Zenobia what he did for Cleopatra. She is first and foremost a historian of the Roman period under investigation in her book. Indeed, she wrote several books on various aspects of this period, such as *Septimius Severus, Philip the Arab, Ghassan Resurrected, The Lakhmids of Hira* and *Echoes of History*. In addition she is a Palestinian, and as such she is a victim of the contending versions of history. Like Zenobia, her everyday life in Palestine reminds her of the cruelty of history and its excesses. Hence she cannot afford, like those who narrated the story of Zenobia before her (notably the late Muhammad Farid Abu-Hadid (1893 – 1967) who wrote in Arabic a highly memorable historical novel on the subject, *Zenobia: Malikat Tadmur,* 1949) to brush history aside. Zahran uses a captivating technique in her book, which provides it, through her multi-layerd narrative, with character and depth. She presents her work initially as a story, narrated in the first person by her heroine, Zenobia; and, at the end of each chapter, provides us with an 'explanatory note' in which she marshals historical evidence for and against the views expressed and the version of events narrated by her heroine. In this section of each chapter Zahran demonstrates her erudition and sensitive methodology as an historian.

Yet, she does not confine her historical investigation of the period to these 'explanatory notes', for she devotes the second half of her book to what one may call a 'total history' of the period and the region. In the last five chapters she provides her reader with a detailed study of the social, political and cultural milieu in which Zenobia lived and within which her story unfolded. She draws the historical background for the period of Zenobia and her husband, Odainat, its contending forces and warring groups, its cultural setting, prevailing ideas, and the various religious groups from the Jews to the early Christians, and from the pan-Hellenists and rationalists to the Manicheans. She also devotes a whole chapter to the story of Zenobia in Arabic tradition and another, one of the most detailed and fascinating, to Tadmur and Palmyra, the city, its culture and religion, its people and their manners, customs and cults. A third chapter is devoted to Palmyran art, its Greco-Oriental characteristics, and how it mediated the Hellenistic influences into Oriental forms and artistic concepts.

But *Zenobia* is not a mere history, it is an exceptional and multi-layered book that owes a great deal of its appeal to its unique form, in which historical account is enhanced by the use of narrative techniques. In the first half of the book, Zahran the novelist takes over, and it is in the body of the first five chapters that she excels. As a narrative she starts her story from the end, so that the tragic end continues to haunt the narrative throughout, and provides it with potency and relevance. She deliberately empowers her heroine, Zenobia, by giving her the right to represent herself, enables her to dominate the narrative perspective, and tell us her own story in her own words. There we see, not how she sees the events and herself, but also how she is seen by others, whose stories about her she is at pain to discuss and purge of their lies. The use of first person narrative enlivens the text, and provides it with drama and potency. Contrary to the stereotype of the Oriental woman, Zenobia emerged as the ablest of women of her time, ambitious, cultured and a symbol of 'women's emancipation', long before the term was coined.

Though she was the most beautiful woman of her time, with long, thick black hair, black eyes that sparkled with fire and teeth so white that many thought she had pearls for teeth, Zenobia did not rely on her beauty alone, and was no idle, languid Oriental seductress, but an ambitious woman who wanted to control the Roman Empire, chaste and virtuous. In the Arabic tradition she was known not to care for men, but to focus more on the affairs of the state, and on securing and expanding her husband's realm and preserving it for her son. She was both cultured and highly determined, had a lavish taste for luxury and royal magnificence, and an insatiable hunger for knowledge and power. The *Historia Augusta* attributes to her the victories of Odainat. Her palace was open to her people who crossed deserts and seas to ask Zenobia for justice and mercy. As a faithful student of Longinus the sublime, she administered her affairs with reason and fairness, succeeded in expanding her kingdom, until she was betrayed, and demonstrated the rationality of Arab women. Although Longinus was a source of sophistication, wisdom and strength, she also perceived him as her Achilles heel, for when Aurelian murdered him, he wounded her.

In narrating the story of Zenobia, an Arab queen from the third century of the Roman Empire, Zahran convincingly argues that the Western misunderstanding and misrepresentation of Arab women is not a recent development. It is a historical phenomenon that goes back to the time of the Roman Empire, and has contributed to the common stereotypes of Arab women today. Her work can be seen as a nuanced and sensitive contribution to the work of her compatriot, Edward Said, on *Orientalism*. As an Arab woman herself, Yasmine Zahran contributes to changing such stereotypes. It may be easy to understand why Zahran, a Palestinian historian and novelist, selected Zenobia as her subject, but the subtle and more pressing question is that of the form. Why did she write her book in this form? The simple answer to this question is that enabling Zenobia to narrate her own story makes her an active contributor to the correction of her story, and shifts the power of representation from the male historian to the female heroine and the female writer. But there is another more significant reason in my reading of the book, and this is that the use of multi-layered narrative, in which she combines history and reality, socio-cultural details and political intrigue, provides the book with a metaphorical edge, and opens it not only to the fight of women to represent themselves and their stories, but also to a metaphorical treatment of the question of Palestine.

Sabry Hafez

Author's Note

The third century of the Roman Empire can be justly called the 'Arab century', in the sense that the Arabs helped to shape Roman history, from the Severan dynasty (193–235), through Philip the Arab (244–249) to Odainat and Zenobia (259–272).

Four Severan emperors, the Empress Julia Domna with her sister and two nieces, followed by Philip the Arab, showered favours on Palmyra, the last Arab stronghold in the East. The other Arab kingdoms and principalities had been crushed and silenced by the Romans; however, none of them had ever reached the military and financial might of Palmyra, nor its potential to build an Arab Empire. Palmyra was a unique phenomenon, where East and West met. It owed its power to being a barrier between the two great empires of Persia and Rome, which allowed it to develop an extensive commercial activity, with trade routes, caravans and trading posts, and poured onto the city untold wealth.

Born in the desert, Palmyra flared brilliantly like a meteor in the sky for six centuries from the third century BC to the third century AD. And then it was gone. However, during the fleeting period of its existence, this small city on the edge of the desert, challenged and shook the very foundations of the two great and mighty empires of the time – Odainat with his smashing victory over the great Persian king and Zenobia over Rome. The destruction of Palmyra closed a historic era for the Arabs in Syria and Mesopotamia and produced a military and commercial vacuum for the Romans, bringing them face to face with Persia and the problems of frontier defence against the incursion of Arab tribes – for Palmyra had controlled the desert frontier all along the Euphrates.

It is astonishing that the rulers of a small desert kingdom took on the two greatest empires the world has known: Odainat fought the Persian Empire and inflicted upon the great king a crushing defeat, and Zenobia took on the Roman Empire, threw the Romans out of the Orient and put them to shame – a sort of dress rehearsal for Odainat's and Zenobia's compatriots, the Arabs of the peninsula who, centuries later, resumed their work, crushing one empire and mutilating the other.

Zenobia, the subject of this study, built an empire which she had seized from the Romans and which extended from the Euphrates to the Bosphorus – a foreshadow of the Umayyad Empire four centuries later. Zenobia and Palmyra, however, are shrouded in legend. To the prejudice of her being a woman in a completely masculine Roman world, and an Oriental, was added excessive romanticism. Her being an Arab queen surprised some historians, but Arab queens existed as early as in the eighth century BC, when Tiglath Pilasar VI (747–727) had had it inscribed in clay 'I received tribute from Zabibe, queen of Arabia'. Another Arab queen of legendary fame, Bilkis, queen of Saba (Sheba) also preceded Zenobia.

Zenobia was a Roman to the Romans, an Arab to the Arabs, a Panhellenist to the Greeks, but in fact she was a Hellenised Arab. Her history, as traced by Western authors, was written by her enemies. On the Arab side, it consists of fantastic legends that concentrate on her feud with the Tanukh, whose storytellers (who were also her enemies) boasted in Arab tents of their victory and her defeat. These Arab legends, unrealistic as they are, contain certain elements of truth and should not be totally ignored.

This present study clarifies certain ambiguous aspects of her life, such as her involvement in philosophy and her devotion to the Platonic ideal, but mainly contests the manner of her death and her humiliation, as reported by her enemies who revelled at her presumed exhibition in the Triumph of Aurelian, while in reality she was already dead. It also dispels, it is hoped, accusations levelled unjustly against her of betraying her Sophist friends. Zenobia was anti-Roman and had great sympathy with Panhellenism, but she was queen of a strong Arab kingdom, with considerable military and financial might, who succeeded in defeating Rome and in establishing a short-lived Arab Empire.

Zenobia, a tragic persona, beautiful, erudite, ambitious, virtuous, courageous, has baffled historians for many centuries. This study portrays her in her own words, the evidence of ancient and modern sources, both Western and Arabic, excavations and research, but it is by no means a historical fiction.

The only and major feat of imagination is Zenobia speaking, and explaining her moves, her life, her death – from the nether world.

Abbreviations

AAS — *Annales Archéologiques Arabes Syriennes*

ADAJ — *Annual of the Department of Antiquities of Jordan*

ANR — *Aufstieg und Niedergang der Römischen Welt*, Berlin 1972–89

CIS — Corpus Inscriptionum Semiticarum, Académie des Inscriptions et Belles Lettres, Paris, 1881–1954. See p. 17

Colloque Arabie — *L'Arabie préislamique et son environnement historique et culturel. Actes du Colloque de Strasbourg 24–27 Juin 1987*, éd. T. FAHD, Université des Sciences humaines de Strasbourg, Travaux du Centre de Recherche sur le Proche-Orient et la Grèce antiques 10, E.J. Brill, Leiden, 1989.

Colloque Palmyre — *Palmyre, Bilan et Perspectives, Colloque de Strasbourg (18–20 Octobre 1973) organisé par le C.R.P.O.G.A. à la mémoire de Daniel Schlumberger et de Henri Seyrig*, Université des Sciences humaines de Strasbourg, Travaux du Centre de Recherche sur le Proche-Orient et la Grèce antiques 3, AECR, Strasbourg, 1976.

Colloque Arabie *L'Arabie préislamique et son environnement historique et culturel. Actes du Colloque de Strasbourg 24–27 juin 1987*, éd. T. FAHD, Université des Sciences humaines de Strasbourg, Travaux du Centre de Recherche sur le Proche-Orient et la Grèce antiques 10, E.J. Brill, Leiden, 1989.

JRS *Journal of Roman Studies*

Supp. Bibl. *Supplément* au *Dictionnaire de la Bible*, Paris

TAPA *Transactions of the American Philological Association*, Philadelphia and Baltimore

CHAPTER I

Fly to the Sun, Zenobia

I, Julia Aurelia Septimia Bat-Zabbaï, al-Zabbâ to the Arabs, Zenobia Sebaste to the Greeks, Augusta to the Romans, most illustrious and pious queen of Tadmur, wife of Odainat, fire breathing lion from the sun[1], *Ras Tadmur,* King of Kings, and mother of Julius Aurelius Septimius Wahaballât, *Imperator Caesar.* I conquered, I vanquished, I subdued, I fought the greatest empire on earth, I swept through ancient cities, I trampled legions and I threw the Romans out of the Orient. I made Palmyra the capital of an empire which extended from the Euphrates to the Bosphorus. My caravans crossed the desert, and their merchandise crossed the seas. I had the key of commercial routes to India and China. I possessed undreamt–of wealth. I gathered in my court the most brilliant, the most luminous intellectuals of the age, but all this satisfied neither my ambitions nor my dreams. I aimed at the Imperial throne of Rome but *HBL*[2], alas, alas, alas, at the summit of my glory,

---

1. Potter, 1990, 151, quotes the thirteenth Sybilline Oracle.
2. Palmyran formula in inscriptions on tombs meaning 'alas' (al-Bounni and al-As'ad, 1987, 108). The term *HBLaTo (HBLTi)* is used to express regret in the area of Ḥoms and Ḥāma until today.

the goddess of destiny Nemesis-Manât[3] crossed my path and darkness fell upon the face of the sun and now I am only the shade of Zenobia. I roam within the dark ocean of the universe, from a cloud of fire to a cloud of ice, from confusion to chaos, from chaos to nothingness. Around me volcanoes spit their rage, mountains split open, seas roar and suddenly become dry. I turn like a wheel amidst the myriad of haunting shades, who, like me, were once part of life. I hear storms raging, winds howling and thunder bellowing, shaking the walls of this anti-universe of which I am now temporarily part.

I call, I pray, I invoke my ancestral gods, and the god 'who hears', 'whose name is blessed forever, who is good and merciful'[4] heard my call and restored to my shade the ability to speak. I was only thirty-two years old when the cycle of my existence stood still. Queen for six years, wife for eighteen years to Odainat, who married me at fourteen and like Pygmalion shaped me into a queen[5].

Ba'alšamîn, the *ra mâna* (merciful), willed me to speak and to put into words the book heavy with joys and sorrows that was my life, before my *naphša* (soul) is allowed to fly to the sun.

My shrivelled body lies deep in the treacherous waters of the Bosphorus, rocked and heaved by rushing angry waves, but if only fate had not intervened I would have been lying

---

3. The Arab goddess Manât was assimilated with Nemesis in Palmyra (Starcky, 1960, 1097).
4. Starcky, 1960, 1097.
5. Zenobia was born in AD 240, married Odainat in 255 and died in 273 (Sartre-Fauriat, 1997, 268).

in our House of Eternity (*BT LM*) at the feet of my beloved Odainat, majestic on his couch of death, to enjoy a survival without resentment or emotion, and only the honours of our descendants[6].

Hear me, Allât 'mother of gods and men'[7]. I am not buried in a tomb, not because I was irreverent to you or to Bêl, the cosmic conqueror of evil, the equal of Zeus[8], nor to his companions, Yarhibôl and 'Aglibôl, gods of the sun and the moon, nor to Rûdâ the benevolent, nor to Arsu and 'Azîzu, morning and evening stars, I never lacked awe for the gods of my Arab ancestry, Rahim, 'Azîzu, Sams, Abgâl and Nebu[9]. Again and again I invoke you Ba'alšamîn, *marê 'alma* (Master of the World), you who reigns over the stars, *hypsistos* (most high). Blessed be your name forever, for I was deprived of the feast of communion for the dead which you would have honoured with your divine presence (Fig. 4). I was deprived of the cake of almonds which would have testified for my afterlife and smoothed my passage to *BT LM*[10].

I call upon you *ginnaya, gad* (local and tribal genie of the place), warrior and protective gods[11], I call upon the twenty-two gods in the Pantheon of Tadmur[12], to tell them that the queen of Tadmur never wavered from their worship. My enemies spread rumours that I renounced you for the faith

---

6. Will, 1992, 120 and 150; Millar, 1996, 132; Stoneman, 1992, 78.
7. Du Mesnil du Buisson, 1962, 372–3.
8. Starcky and Gawlikowski, 1985, 108.
9. Dussaud, 1957, 90–1.
10. Starcky, 1960, 1101.
11. Starcky, 1960, 1100–01; Stoneman, 1992, 67.
12. 'Alī, 1968–73, 130.

of the Christians and the Jews, even for Manicheism[13], but I followed your rituals and never missed drinking wine at the sacred meal (*marzeha*), nor the ritual washing before the meal[14]. Neither soldiering, nor philosophical speculation ever stood between me and my gods.

I cannot rest, for my body does not lie in the tomb my husband built within the city walls, a privilege for the family of Odainat[15]. I wanted a funerary tower, like those scattered majestically on the southern tip of the city – haunting in the harmony of their towering lines and more beautiful than the temples of Bêl, Nabu and Ba'alšamîn, more fascinating than the colonnaded street and the elegant palaces. How I envied the dead inhabitants of those towers with their many floors, looming high on the clear horizon, an abode that spoke loudly of the loneliness of death. Odainat al-Zabbā' ridiculed my passion. 'Al-Zabbā', he would say, 'I thought it is life and not death that obsesses you. Your funerary towers are things of the past, for no tower was built in Tadmur in the last one hundred and fifty years, and if you don't like our tomb you could join a burial club and pay a subscription to ensure you lodgement after death[16], or better still you could be buried like a common person in a pit in the desert!' Did Odainat, I wonder, realise how prophetic were his words, for I did not even achieve a burial in a pit of hot sands, in a burning desert? Instead, I lie in the cold, cold waters of a slimy sea.

---

13. Starcky, 1960, 1098.
14. Stoneman, 1992, 73.
15. Stoneman, 1992, 67–8.
16. Browning, 1979, 201.

I remembered these words after Odainat's assassination, when I regularly visited his tomb, and contemplated the niche reserved for my burial – and my sculpture which will lie at his feet in a funerary banquet. I wonder where they scattered his bones when Aurelian's soldiers sacked and plundered the city and ravaged his tomb. We both lost repose in our House of Eternity, his bones rotting somewhere in the sands and mine dissolving in their bed of water in a hostile sea.

There is nothing left of his tomb – the sculptures were wrecked. But I am told that the inscription remains: '*This sepulchre was constructed by Septimius Odainat, the Clarissimus Senator, son of airân, son of Wahaballât, son of Nasôr, for himself and his sons and the sons of his sons for always, in eternal honour*'[17].

But, alas, I have no tomb, not even a funerary stele (*naphša*), symbol and memorial of the dead. My body was not mummified and nothing is left of my material existence. I can only wait for the promise of a timeless life, when my soul will be transported to the hereafter and live in the sun[18].

In life I was annoyed by the excessive Palmyran preoccupation with the afterlife, until I conquered Egypt and found that it was nothing compared to that of the Egyptians[19], and, now being on the other side of life, I am obsessed with the thousands and thousands of Palmyrans in the prime of their youth whom I sent to war and who lie

---

17. Will, 1992, 194.
18. Starcky and Gawlikowski, 1985, 110–11.
19. Browning, 1979, 206.

scattered, without burial, under the cruel elements in the battlefields of Asia, Syria and Egypt.

I am obliged to continue to speak until I shed light on the layers of ambition, courage, vanity, deceit, intrigue, luxury, revenge, love and hate that once made up Zenobia – and I shall begin in reverse, at omega point, my defeat and captivity – for in my blindness I never believed I could be defeated. I had confidence in the strength of my armies, and the vast resources of the empire which I built. Aurelian recaptured Egypt and Asia Minor and followed my retreating army. After my defeats at Immae, near Antioch, and Emesa, I retreated with the remnants of the army to Palmyra which was fortified – our last refuge. Aurelian followed and besieged the city, but I still believed in victory and awaited Persian help. I remembered Odainat's words when I harassed him at the height of his power to attack the Romans. 'Al-Zabbā', he said, 'there are two great empires in the world. I took on one, Persia, but I cannot take on two'. He left it for me to challenge Rome.

I took on Rome, but ironically expected help from the former enemy[20]. Zabadas, my general-commander, and I tried to prolong the siege, to lengthen the war in the hope that the Persians would come to our aid, but our situation was very grave, the *plebs* and the horde of immigrants who thrived on our prosperity were now clamouring for capitulation. The nobility were adamant not to surrender – except for the Symposiarch Septimius Haddûdân[21], the

---

20. Cizek, 1994, 109.
21. Will, 1992, 194; Sartre-Fauriat, 1997, 271.

chief priest of Bêl, who headed the party for capitulation. To think that a man I had appointed to the highest religious function less than a year before, and who bore the *gentilice* Septimius as a mark of honour given only to a few outside the royal family, would turn into a traitor! He hoped, perhaps, by treason to save the State Treasury and other private treasures deposited for safe keeping in the temple of Bêl. Provisions were getting scarce, the Arab tribes and the Armenian allies had been repelled and could not come to our assistance. Our enemies the Tanūkh were fighting alongside the army of Aurelian[22]. I held a limited war council which decided that I should go to the Euphrates and cross over to the Persian lines to seek aid. The idea was to convince the Persians to attack Syria, while Roman and Egyptian troops were concentrated around Palmyra.

Such a diversion, I was sure, would compel Aurelian to lift the siege[23]. I sneaked out of the city at night, with a contingent of light troops. We drove our camels to death until we reached the bank of the Euphrates, and, as I was about to embark on a waiting boat to cross to the other bank, the cavalry of Aurelian arrived and took us captives to his camp[24]. How can I speak of that moment, with hardly a margin between hope and despair? All was lost, there was no relief, nor hope, for Tadmur. In fact, the city surrendered after a few days and the news was brought to me by my

---

22. *Historia Augusta, Divus Aurelianus,* 11.3; Shahîd, 1984a, 24.
23. Février, 1931, 134.
24. *Hist. Aug., Aurel.,* 28, 3; Zosimus, *Historia Nova,* 54, 4 and 55, 2–3.

enemies that my son Wahaballât, *Augustus* and King of Kings, true to his ancestors and his gods, had fallen fighting the Romans at the gates of Tadmur[25]. I was also told how the avid Aurelian put his hands on our riches, a wealth beyond measure gathered over the centuries. He took both the state treasure and my private royal treasure (money, precious stones, gold, silk, horses and camels) to the Roman Treasury, and the city was given over to the sack and loot by his soldiers.

For me, Zenobia, there was only one thing left. I had said before that the last moment of my life and reign should be the same[26], and I had written to Aurelian, in answer to his impudent letter which he sent me during the siege, asking me to surrender, that I was no less than Cleopatra who preferred to die than to surrender[27]. Faced now with the implication and the horror of the catastrophe, the crumbling of the empire I built, the destruction of my beloved city, the end of my world, I revelled in the relief that death and death alone could restore my liberty, and offer me access to immortality.

Bound in chains, I was brought before Aurelian in Emesa, where he had returned after the rape of Tadmur. My face betrayed nothing of my agony, my composure was not unworthy of my ancestors the Septimii. I was no longer in a position to shape my life, but I did not degrade it nor unnecessarily expose it to Roman cruelty. I said to myself:

---

25. Hitti, 1951, 440.
26. Gibbon, 1934, 265.
27. *Hist. Aug., Aurel.,* 27, 3, 5.

'Zenobia, you are the last Arab queen and you will join the kings and princes of Iturea, Nabatea, Edessa, Emesa and Hatra – all crushed by the Romans.' My only sadness was that with me would die the yearnings of the Arabs for independence and freedom for centuries to come, and that my dream of the imperial throne of Rome had turned to dust and ashes.

I had lost everything, only one thing remained, but I had not taken into account Aurelian's vigilance, for he well understood my desire for death and since he wanted to preserve me for his Triumph, he had me watched day and night. Zenobia, the fallen star, defeated and humiliated, was to be exhibited to the Roman *plebs*, for, according to the senator and author Cassius Dio, the humiliation of the rich and privileged was said to be a source of enormous pleasure to the common people[28]. That was to be the epitome of his career. He wanted Zenobia crushed and broken in order to avenge the derision he had aroused in the Senate and the Roman public for fighting a woman as his opponent. They had accused him of unmanly behaviour, trampling on a woman!

I had not forgotten the shock I had given the Romans for being a general at the head of my troops, for Roman women in the upper classes had wealth and influence, but no political roles, limited legal rights and were, moreover, the objects of misogynist invective and of an ideology that rewarded female subservience[29].

---

28. Hallett and Skinner, 1998, 86.
29. Hallett and Skinner, 1998, 236.

Abysmal as the situation was, I had a lingering hope when I learnt that the situation was not easy for Aurelian: the hostilities with the Persians had continued and he had not even attempted to reconquer lost Mesopotamia. My allies, the Armenians, refused to return to the sovereignty of Rome. I also knew that neither the Palmyrans nor the Egyptians, who had tasted freedom under our rule, would remain long under the Roman yoke.

Aurelian was in a hurry to return to the West, for the Carpes were attacking Moesea[30] and he planned to take me with him, as well as the Palmyrans who refused to surrender[31], and who had participated in what he termed the 'Revolt'.

He kept me isolated and watched, but I knew that his soldiers were clamouring for my death[32] while he insisted on keeping his trophy alive.

One day I heard the slaves who brought my food, whispering, and one of them was sobbing aloud. When I enquired as to the reason for this, they started wailing and said that the emperor had just executed the Sophist Cassius Longinus and with him all my advisors, generals and other aides. I stood staring at the window and said nothing. I did not know how long I remained in that position. I thought I had drunk the cup of sorrow to the full, but the abyss of sorrow is bottomless.

Aurelian carried me with him and paraded me through

---

30. Homo, 1904, 105–08.
31. Zosimus, *Historia Nova*, 1, 56, 1 and 59, 1.
32. *Hist. Aug., Aurel.,* 30, 1, 2.

the streets and hippodrome of Antioch[33] as a foretaste of his Triumph in Rome, and, after dragging me and the Palmyrans through the cities of Asia Minor, he put me on his imperial ship, while the Palmyran prisoners were put on another, for they were also to be paraded in his Triumph.

Aurelian was terrified and haunted by the possibility of my suicide. My rings were searched for poison and taken away, and my cabin was ceaselessly searched for instruments with which I could open my veins. He tried all means at his disposal to humiliate me, but it seems that this was not enough. He could not overcome a vindictiveness that rankled because I had made Wahaballât *Augustus*, a title that only he, Aurelian, should have borne, as he alone should wear the radiating crown which made him the earthly representative of a supreme god[34]. He bitterly resented sharing the empire with Wahaballât, because I had coins struck in Antioch with Aurelian's portrait on the reverse.

Aurelian carried with him on the ship part of my royal treasury, my jewels and state robes, in which I was to be bedecked for his Triumph. 'I ordered golden chains for you', he said with a sardonic grimace, 'It is the least I can do for the dark-haired beauty, the queen of the desert, the pretender *Augusta*, who has dared to aspire to the imperial throne!'

One evening he came to my cabin with a slave carrying my jewels (Figs. 5, 6 and 7) on a tray and asked me with an innocent air which necklace I preferred to wear to the Triumph, the one with emeralds as big as partridge eggs or

33. Watson, 1998, 79.
34. Février, 1931, 115.

the one with rubies from the heart of India. I did not avert my eyes from my jewels, the most precious being those that Odainat had carried from the sack of the tent of the retreating great king[35] and others which I had picked from every caravan, for the merchants gave me the first choice of jewels, perfumes and silks from China, India, Babylon, Characne and beyond. I remembered all the wealth that poured into our desert city. I heard again the clamour and bustle of loading the caravans for the great yearly voyage. I saw the crowd of merchants at the Agora, bargaining, shouting, laughing. I saw the crowd of women and children saying goodbye – for the voyage, despite all precautions, held multiple dangers, and the invocations of the gods for the merchants' safety were so intense that they reached the heavens. No wonder that some gods were militarised – cavalier gods on horse and camel in military garb like Arsu and Abgâl[36] – so as to guide the caravans to safety through all the unforeseen dangers lurking in the crossing of the desert. Aurelian was irritated by my non-reaction to the jewels he knew I loved and went on to describe to me how the Roman *plebs* would gape at the jewels and how the wily senators would gaze with controlled greed. The subject of the senators infuriated him, because they only showed contempt for his fighting and triumphing over a woman whose husband had defended the empire against the Persians[37]. Besides, he knew how they would deplore the

---

35. Gibbon, 1934, 237.
36. Starcky and Gawlikowski, 1985, 111; Will, 1992, 104.
37. Starcky and Gawlikowski, 1985, 68.

humiliation inflicted against one of their class, for was I not a Roman senator's wife?

He implored me to speak, but what could I say? – that the jewels had become only coloured glass, and my silk, embroidered state robes only rags. I did break, however, my silence once and asked him: 'How could you have a Triumph, when you considered Palmyra part and parcel of the Roman Empire? Triumphs, as Roman tradition decrees, are celebrations of victory against external and foreign enemies – Septimius Severus did not celebrate his victories in two civil wars against Niger and Albinus.'

He cut me short and flew into a rage, covering up his flouting of Roman traditions by shouting: 'Do you think I am ignorant?', but I did not answer. I already regretted my jibe, for any dialogue with him was beneath my dignity, my being a Hellenised Arab aristocrat, and he only an uncouth barbarian with nothing Roman about him except his military tunic!

The news of an uprising in Palmyra and Egypt did not come. I knew it was in the making, but how long could I wait? The scales were tipped when I learnt that the ship carrying the Palmyran captives had sunk in the storm that hit us in the straits of the Bosphorus, but a perverse fate had allowed the imperial ship to escape.

My hour had come. I could indulge no longer in the chimera that Tadmur would rise again, but the means for taking my life before reaching Rome were lacking, except for one. I decided on suicide by starvation[38], just like my idol

---

38. Zosimus, *Hist. Nov.*, 1, 59, 1.

Julia Domna, and for the second time in my life I stood in opposition to fate. The first time, I had not heeded the oracles that were unfavourable to the war against the Romans. As usual, before going to war, I had consulted two oracles, Apollo of Sarpedon in Cilician Seleucia and Aphacan Venus in Syria. The replies of both were unfavourable and implied disastrous results[39], but I defied fate. The second occasion was my deciding to commit suicide against the will of the gods.

The adventure of my life was ending. All the elemental furies had turned against me with malice, tearing me out of a lingering hope for the Palmyran uprising. Thus, I began the process of annihilation and of sweeping the world utterly out of my sight.

Starvation is a very slow way to death, especially for a healthy young body, the first days being the most painful, as I felt the pangs of hunger very acutely. But with abstinence my mind began to clear, for I was moving into another level of being. My regrets were ebbing out, and, slowly, hidden layers in myself steeped in darkness made their appearance. At the heart of darkness was loneliness. How can I explain the loneliness of the soul before the unknown, for whatever the Sophists and the gods had taught me had not prepared me for facing the void?

It is difficult to be no more – not to hear war cries of my desert troops. Even though I was seeking death, I realised that the mere fact of living is the greatest thing that the gods had given me. Life that bubbles and flows, life which is

---

39. Février, 1931, 120.

ecstatic and full of sorrow – but sorrow is sweet. There are moments when the memories and desires of a once-healthy body plague me, the smell of a rose, the odour of a perfume made of a thousand flowers that hypnotises my senses, the sensual touch of my silk robe, the flashing of a gem on my finger (Fig. 8), riding with a haze of heat caressing my face. Yet, I have suddenly realized that my body has aged. I am now what I would be if I lived to be old – old age is a land that leads nowhere, a land without a future, without joy. A lament rises in my throat for all the beautiful young bodies cut in their prime on the battlefields, but who at least did not have to face the indignities of the dissolution of their carnal bodies.

In life I had longed at times for solitude – a luxury of the spirit –, for loneliness is a malediction that did not afflict me. I was always surrounded by people I loved: my family, my tribe, my generals, my philosophers, my partisans and above all, my soldiers. In a way I was an amalgam of all these people. I helped them fulfil their dreams of glory, of glamour, of adventure. They in turn padded me against loneliness, but I let them down. I destroyed their world and in the process destroyed them. Now, I suddenly realised that I existed not only in relation to my friends, but more so in relation to my enemies, for every act of mine was measured by its reflection on them. My loneliness was not only for people, but for the familiar landscape, for the magic city (Fig. 2) with its temples and honeyed colonnades, for the hills surrounding Palmyra with their stud and camel farms whose lush green contrasted with the desert, and for its dawns of silvery mist. From my narrow porthole I sometimes have a glimpse of the moon on the water and my heart aches for the crescent moon rising above the temple of Bêl. I sigh and scream, knowing that no one will hear me: 'You destroyed all that you loved, Zenobia', and I murmur in self-defence, 'I only continued the work of Odainat on the foundations that he built before they so cruelly cut his life.'

Hunger makes the days seem longer and, oh, so empty. How I long for the days that are gone, marriage, childbearing, riding, hunting, campaigning with Odainat and then on my own – awaiting the arrival of caravans at dusk (Fig. 9), meeting with the soldiers who man our forts along the Euphrates, some of which I have built myself[40], war councils with Generals Zabadas and Zabbaï, reviewing, parading and banqueting with my soldiers, waiting for the pleasure of the evenings with my Sophists, when, adorned, bejewelled and perfumed, I sat on silk-embroidered couches with my historians and poets (Fig. 10), discussing with my Sophists the secrets of the self and the universe, while nectar in cups studded with precious stones was served by my handsome young eunuch slaves.

It was amusing how my Sophists would question me on my meetings with one or the other colleges of priests attached to the various temples. They wanted to hear about the theological astral system and the transcendental conception of the divine which reaches out towards the concept of the One, Unknown god, but I refused, saying they must go themselves and ask the questions. The only nights I was away from my Sophists were when

---

40. Février, 1931, 115–16; Sartre-Fauriat, 1997, 269.

I was banqueting with my Arab kin, who rode across the desert and reported to me the latest schemes and intrigues of my arch-enemies the Tanūkh, who were forever conspiring to replace us as the lords of the desert. After the banquet I loved exchanging with them Arabic proverbs and tales, but my greatest pleasure came at the close of the evening, when the poets began their competition for the recital of the best poem. I often refused to be the judge, fearing the poets' enmity and satire more than an enemy on the battlefield.

My mornings were spent in the town council, dealing with town planning, permits for the building of new temples and permits for tombs, and I often received members of the Jewish and Christian communities who were always asking for special favours. Odainat had given the Christians their freedom to practise their rites and allowed them to build churches while they were persecuted elsewhere.

Aurelian was thunderstruck when he learnt of my hunger strike. He sent me trays of delicacies from his table, which were returned untouched. My ankles and wrists became too thin to hold the chains which he ordered removed. He came at last to harangue me: 'Who is the general who fought Roman legions now a coward who does not accept her fate? Is that the exuberant queen who not only outdrank her soldiers, but the Persian and Armenian generals until they rolled under the table?'.

He looked, mesmerised, at my shrunken body, at my haggard face which once the world thought beautiful, at my lustreless, half-closed eyes, whose luminosity poets once sang, at my hair turned suddenly grey which once was black reflecting the sun, my body strengthened by riding and hunting and fighting, now a bent skeleton. He left my cabin troubled and sent his doctors bidding them to keep me alive. 'She cannot die, she must not die', he shouted. I must not be allowed to die, for that would take away his sweet revenge, for the humiliation I inflicted upon him was still fresh. How could he forget that I absolutely controlled for five years the richest provinces of the empire, and that I held the routes of India, through Egypt and through Syria[41]? How could he forget that I conquered Egypt when the wheat-bearing fleet was about to sail to Rome and that he could have faced a hunger revolt in the capital? He could not forget I had controlled a great part of Asia Minor and was planning to seize Bithynia, cross the Bosphorus to Thrace and aimed at placing Wahaballât in place of Elagabalus[42] on the imperial throne. I never made a secret of Rome being my ultimate goal, whereas my husband had never envisaged such an audacious venture[43].

Aurelian alternated his threats with promises: I would not be beheaded as the tradition decrees, but would be granted the life of a Roman matron with a villa in Tibur, and not only that, but a noble Roman husband as well[44]. He was sick with delusions. 'You must be in the Triumph', he said, and boasted of the wild beasts – twenty elephants, four

---

41. Ingholt, 109; *Hist. Aug., Tyranni Triginta*, 25, 18.
42. Février, 1931, 117.
43. Hadas, 1958, 137; 'Alī, 1968–73, 127.
44. *Hist. Aug. Aurel.*, 2, 4, 20; 33; 34, 3; *Hist. Aug. Tyr. Trig.*, 30; Starcky and Gawlikowski, 1985, 67.

tigers, two hundred curious animals, one thousand and six hundred gladiators, ambassadors from Ethiopia, Arabia, Bactria, India and China. But when he mentioned an ambassador from Persia, I chuckled weakly and I thought he must be deranged. He then spoke of crowns of gold offered by the cities, and of the hordes of prisoners, Goths, Vandals, Sarmatians, Alemani, Franks, Gauls, Syrians and Egyptians who would march behind him; and the chariots, that of Odainat wrought in gold and silver, the chariot which I built to enter Rome and a chariot which was a present from the king of Persia. 'You will be the star, Zenobia, and if the golden chains are too heavy, there will be a Persian buffoon to help you with the chains.'[45]

I was too weak to laugh at his megalomania. To think that he imagined that the king of Persia would send him a chariot and an ambassador to walk in his Triumph was as mad and unrealistic as imagining that I who was so near to death, would walk in his procession in golden chains!

He tried a method other than threats, and he talked calmly trying to reason with me, that he was giving me my life, and after all was there anything more important than life? But how could I explain to him that when sorrows accumulate they go beyond reason, beyond grief to a corner in ourselves with no issues and no doors, and that a loss like mine triggers an abstraction which foregoes desire itself; the soul is naked before the gods and wishes nothing but release.

---

45. *Hist. Aug., Aurel.,* 33; *Hist. Aug., Tyr. Trig.,* 30; Hadas, 1958, 136–7; Will, 1992, 195.

His megalomania and his delusions, however, sparked in the diminished state of my mind the memories of my own illusions, for my main delusion was for power and when I realised it, the anticlimax was shattering. All my life I had dreamt of controlling the most brilliant, most intellectual city of the empire – Alexandria, the seat of philosophers, teachers, theologians and artists. Not a nominal control as Odainat had over Egypt, but a real one, and toward this end I studied Egyptian. I built my military power and spread the rumour that I was a descendant of Cleopatra, which now seems to me grotesque, but when I did enter the dreamt-of Alexandria, the Alexandria of mind and spirit, victorious at the head of my army, welcomed and acclaimed by Alexandrians as their liberator from the oppression of the Romans, at that moment so long desired I felt nothing but dust and ashes – for all ambitions when fulfilled, become chaff in the wind. I play-acted. Neither my entourage nor the Alexandrian dignitaries detected my sadness at the futility and absurdity of things.

Aurelian came for the last time bringing with him doctors who had been ordered to 'feed her by force, keep her alive', and then he turned to me disgusted by my swollen face and said in a pathetic voice of a man, not that of an emperor: 'Zenobia, all your life you were a glittering star, first in beauty, virtue and courage, but you will also be the first in my Triumph. The world will not be looking at Aurelian but at Zenobia, the star, the fallen star.'

How he fatigued me with his threats and pleas, but deliverance was near, my soul was escaping my discarded body. I heard Aurelian's head beating on the door of my cabin. There was a rattle in his throat, as in that of a hunter who has just missed his prey, for his victim had eluded him. And then the order: 'She is dead, throw her into the sea'. They did, but when my bloated body began to sink, I heard Odainat's words: 'Al-Zabbā' (for he only used my Arabic name), 'you were always gazing at the fountains I built for you; water hypnotises you. You have such thirst for water, like all those born of the desert.' I heard him chuckling, 'Now you will have all the water you want.'

The last images were emitting from my dying feverish brain. I saw myself riding beside Odainat, pursuing the Persian army, for I was always at his side, whether for the hunt or for war. Odainat stands before me, his lips move, but I cannot hear what he says. I see him in all his splendour, an Arab chief, a King of Kings, and faintly I heard the barbarian haranguing the physicians: 'Idiots, fools, slaves, why did you let her die?'

I am now only a shadow, floating over all the places I once knew as I have no House of Eternity, my body is cradled and rocked by the deep, deep water of a foreign sea, but I shall continue to speak, until my *naphša* (soul), as promised, will fly to live in the sun.

Explanatory Note:

Zenobia's Suicide

Western historiographical tradition on Zenobia was compiled and transmitted by Westerners – the case of the victor writing the story of his enemy. Graeco-Roman historians writing long after the death of Zenobia gathered shreds of information, sometimes of doubtful origin, concerning her fate after the defeat, and produced different versions[1].

The most prevalent and popular version is that of Aurelius Victor who wrote the *Historia Augusta* ca AD 395 in the reign of Theodosius (thus one hundred and twenty-two years after Zenobia's death), and ascribed it to six historians. Ronald Syme has demonstrated that it was written by a single hand, that of Aurelius Victor[2]. His version[3] claims that Aurelian reprieved Zenobia, and carried her to Rome where she appeared in his triumphal procession in gold chains and flashing with jewels. He also gave her a villa in Tibur (Tivoli) and a noble Roman husband[4]. She was supposed to have left descendants in Italy, one of them the Bishop of Florence[5]. This version was followed by modern historians, and more recently also by some archaeologists. Other versions claimed that Aurelian

---

1. Gagé, 1964, 397.
2. Stoneman, 1992, 9–10 refers to Syme, 1983, 209–23.
3. Commentary by Paschoud, 1996b, 162 on *Hist. Aug., Aurel.,* 34.3.
4. *Hist. Aug., Tyr. Trig.,* 27, 2.
5. Eutropius, *Breviarum,* 9, 3; Gibbon, 1934, 270.

married one of her daughters[6]. There is no record, however, that Zenobia had any daughters[7].

The sixth-century *Chronicon* of John Malalas states that Zenobia was beheaded after the Triumph[8].

The most reliable account of the history of the Roman Empire from Augustus to AD 410, was written by Zosimus at the end of the fifth century, and, although he generally corroborates the sequence of events in the *Historia Augusta*, he differs radically on the question of Zenobia's death. According to him, Zenobia died on her way to Rome by illness or suicide by starvation[9]. Both versions were mentioned by Zonaras in the twelfth century[10]. However, it was the version put forward by the *Historia Augusta* of Zenobia alive and humiliated in the triumphal procession, that was followed in full or in part by Classical authors, Festus, Eutropius and St Jerome, and by a series of modern writers[11].

This picture, created by the fantasy of Aurelius Victor, appealed to the Roman public. In their arrogance, the Romans were outraged that an Arab queen had dared challenge the might of Rome and were flattered by her defeat. It was also part of Roman propaganda that Rome was invincible. The tragedy of Zenobia's fall also appealed

---

6.   Sartre-Fauriat, 1997, 272, n. 1.
7.   Schwartz, 1976, 150.
8.   Malalas, *Chronicon* XII.
9.   Zos. *Hist. Nov.,* 1, 59.
10. Zonaras, *Annales,* I, 12, 47–8.
11. Gibbon, 1934, 269; 'Alī, 1968–73, 120; Stoneman, 1992, 181–2; Homo, 1904, 123; Starcky and Gawlikowski, 1985, 67–8.

to the perverse side of human character which enjoys the misfortunes of others. Here was a woman who had beauty, learning, courage, virtue and power, who realized her ambitions but could not escape Nemesis.

But why did so many modern authors follow the version of the *Historia Augusta* and not that of Zosimus? L. Homo answers this question by attributing Zosimus' version to an Oriental tradition which according to him is wrong. That a tradition is wrong because it is Oriental as opposed to Western, is, to say the least, curious, considering that Zenobia was an Oriental queen, and that the Orient most likely transmitted a more credible version of her end. After mentioning Zosimus' version and Zonaras' two versions, A. Watson suggests that Zosimus must have invented the story – a hypothesis confirmed by all other literary sources, both ancient and modern. Thus, Zosimus' version must be rejected[12].

The Arab historical tradition accords with Zosimus' claim that she committed suicide. This tradition ignores the Romans, and attributes Zenobia's defeat to her enemies, the federation of the Tanūkh, through tricks and treachery. When her enemies stormed the city, she tried to escape through a secret tunnel, but came face to face with 'Amr b. 'Adī, who blocked the door. When Zenobia recognised him she committed suicide by sucking her poisoned ring and saying the famous phrase, which became an Arab proverb: 'By my hand [I die] and not by yours 'Amr.' This version is

---

12. Homo, 1904, 124, n. 3; Watson, 1998, 83.

mentioned by al-Ṭabari and followed by the major Arab historians[13].

The final proof of Zenobia's suicide lies in her character. She admired Cleopatra who preferred to die rather than to surrender[14]. This statement is mentioned, strangely enough, in the *Historia Augusta* in Zenobia's reply to Aurelian's letter asking her to surrender. She also admired and idealised Julia Domna, the Arab empress from Emesa who committed suicide by starvation in Antioch, when her son the Emperor Caracalla, was assassinated. It is difficult to envisage Zenobia with her excessive pride accepting a reprieve by Aurelian and the humiliation of being dragged in his Triumph. It is completely out of character for a woman who conquered the wealthier half of the Roman Empire and who claimed for her son and for herself the imperial throne, to allow herself to be thus degraded.

Our study follows Zosimus' version, because it is generally agreed that he was better informed and more reliable than Aurelius Victor, described by Syme as sly and silly, a collector with an untidy mind[15]. The latter's version, moreover, is full of discrepancies, and his sources are imaginary[16]. The *Historia Augusta* is full of fakes such as Aurelian's letter to Macapor describing the difficult siege of

---

13. Al-Ṭabarī, *Ta'rikh al-Rusul*, Vol. 1, 448–9; al-Ya'ḳūbī, *al-Kāmil*, Vol. 2, 209; al-Iṣfahānī, *Kitāb al-Aghāni*, Vol. 15, 256; al-Ma'sūdī, *Murūdj*, Vol. 2, 21; al-Ḳazwīnī, *Āthār*, 425.

14. *Hist. Aug., Aurel.*, 27, 1.

15. Stoneman, 1992, 9–10.

16. Schwartz, 1976, 150.

Tadmur[17], as well as fictitious documents[18]. According to Aurelius Victor, Persian prisoners walked in the triumphal processions[19] and one of the chariots was a present from the Persian king. It is difficult to envisage that the traditional enemy and the late ally of Zenobia would present such a gift to Aurelian on his Triumph[20]. Another impossibility is that Zenobia, a captive, vanquished and exhibited, would enter the triumphal procession in the chariot on which she had prepared herself to enter Rome as a conqueror[21]. Furthermore, would the Roman emperor ride in a barbarian chariot, that of the king of the Goths[22]?

The *Historia Augusta* describes the Triumph in detail[23]. The description is admittedly dazzling with exotic animals, gladiators and ambassadors. It was thought by Eutropius to have been remarkable[24]. Grotesque, however, is the very idea that Zenobia should have accepted Aurelian's reprieve, and, after walking in chains in his Triumph, that she should have ended her life as a Roman matron in provincial Tibur. Surely, this is a story invented by the *Historia Augusta*.

Aurelian may have had his dazzling Triumph, but Zenobia was not there!

---

17. *Hist. Aug., Aurel.*, 4, 5, 3.
18. Gagé, 1964, 347.
19. *Hist. Aug., Aurel.*, 28, 2, 4.
20. Commentary on *Historia Augusta, Divus Aurelianus*, by Paschoud, 1996b, 162.
21. *Hist. Aug., Aurel.*, 32, 4.
22. Stoneman, 1992, 182.
23. *Hist. Aug., Tyr. Trig.*, 30; *Hist. Aug., Aurel.*, 32, 4, and 33, 1, 2.
24. Eutrop., *Brev.*, 9, 13.

Fig. 2   General view of the city of Tadmur-Palmyra from the south-west, with the Sanctuary of Nebu in the foreground (Courtesy of the Ministry of Tourism of the Syrian Arab Republic)

Fig. 3   The oasis of Palmyra (Photo Julien Charlopin)

Fig. 4   Limestone low-relief carving (l 19 cm; w 13 cm) depicting the holy triad, Baʿalšamîn in the centre flanked by ʿAglibôl and Malakbôl, ca AD 50, National Archaeological Museum, Damascus (Courtesy of the General Directorate of Antiquities and Museums of the Syrian Arab Republic)

Fig. 5   Pair of golden earrings (h 4 cm; w. 5.8 cm; Th. 0.8 cm), second century AD, National Archaeological Museum, Damascus (Courtesy of the General Directorate of Antiquities and Museums of the Syrian Arab Republic)

Fig. 6   Golden brooch (h 11.8 cm; diam. 4.4 cm), mid-second century AD, National Archaeological Museum, Damascus (Courtesy of the General Directorate of Antiquities and Museums of the Syrian Arab Republic)

Fig. 7   Golden earring (h 6 cm; diam. 2.4 cm), first to second century AD, National Archaeological Museum, Damascus (Courtesy of the General Directorate of Antiquities and Museums of the Syrian Arab Republic)

Fig. 8   Hand and wrist of a female statue in painted stucco (l 15 cm; w 9 cm), second to third century AD, Palmyra Museum (Courtesy of the General Directorate of Antiquities and Museums of the Syrian Arab Republic)

Fig. 9   Hard, white limestone low-relief carving (h 30 cm; l 45 cm) depicting two camel-drivers, early second century AD, National Archaeological Museum, Damascus (Courtesy of the General Directorate of Antiquities and Museums of the Syrian Arab Republic)

Fig. 10   White marble funerary stele (h 53 cm; l 82 cm; d 11 cm) of Malê and Bôlayâ, late second century AD, National Archaeological Museum, Damascus (Courtesy of the General Directorate of Antiquities and Museums of the Syrian Arab Republic)

Fig. 11 Low-relief carving on one of the beams of the Temple of Bêl depicting Palmyran deities as warriors (Photo Julien Charlopin)

Fig. 12 The Valley of Tombs (Photo Studio Zouhabi, Palmyra)

Fig. 13 On the edge of the city of Tadmur-Palmyra, with the Valley of Tombs in the distance (Photo Studio Zouhabi, Palmyra)

Fig. 14 Bilingual (Greek and Palmyran) inscription on the entrance-lintel of Odainat's tomb (Photo Studio Zouhabi, Palmyra)

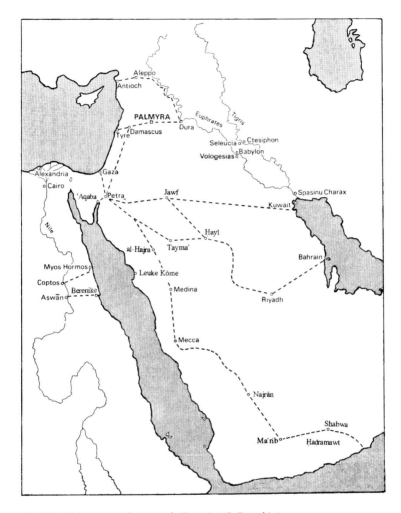

Fig. 15   Palmyra's trade network (Drawing C. Dauphin)

Fig. 16 Dedicatory inscription to Septimius Odaenathus on a column of the Great Colonnade in Tadmur-Palmyra (Photo Studio Zouhabi, Palmyra)

Fig. 17 Dedicatory inscription to Septimia Zenobia on a column of the Great Colonnade in Tadmur-Palmyra (Photo Studio Zouhabi, Palmyra)

Chapter II

Longinus the Sublime

There are myriad kinds of love. My love for Cassius Longinus was a thirst for beauty, a search for truth, an overture for joy, an intellectual exercise on the essence of existence, an intensity of being. He had the keys of the spirit, beyond the world of appearance and possibly to the heart of the universe. For all this I loved him; he was my teacher, my mentor, the architect of my ambition, my chief counsellor, the conductor of my diplomacy with Rome, my confidant and my friend.

In the outer forms of things, we were worlds apart, Longinus and I. He, the philosopher, the former head of the Academy of Athens[1] whose reputation preceded him to Palmyra (his works were numerous, mainly on Plato and Homer), and I the young immature bride of Odainat, the great Arabian chief whose hospitable court was open to remarkable men of all creeds and to which Longinus sought refuge after the sack of the Aegean Islands and Athens by the Goths[2] in AD 267. Between us also stood age. Longinus

---

1. Millar, 1969, 16; Loriot and Nony, 1997, 252.
2. Février, 1931, 106; Hadas, 1958, 135.

was thirty years my senior and ten years older than my husband[3].

I was young, curious and avid for learning. Odainat was training me for war. I accompanied him in his military exercises with the army and later on in his campaigns. I rode and hunted with him, but he left me with Longinus for the study of philosophy, rhetoric and languages. My Arabic was good, and so was my Aramaic, the official language of Palmyra, but my Latin was bad. I understood from the beginning that he came to our court to gather support for the renaissance of Panhellenism[4] and that he was inherently and violently anti-Roman, so we gave out that he came to instruct the court in Greek[5]. In a way Palmyra was near to his roots, for his mother was Syrian from Emesa, sister of the Sophist Fronto. One of his first acts at court was to write a panegyric on Odainat, which he used a short time after, alas, as a funeral oration on Odainat's death and which is now lost[6]. On Odainat's assassination, when my world was turned upside down, and Palmyra faced chaos, I leant more and more on him; he helped me smooth the succession of my son Wahaballât and assume the regency. I did nothing without his advice for he was a man infinitely cultivated, a living library and a museum, in the Alexandrian sense of a university[7]. These were black days

---

3. Longinus was born in AD 210, Zenobia in 241 and Odainat in 220.
4. Zos., *Hist. Nov.*, 57.
5. Sirinelli, 1995, 428.
6. Sartre-Fauriat, 1997, 273.
7. Sirinelli, 1995, 427 and 430.

that followed Odainat's death, for his military and diplomatic achievements were in danger. There was a vacuum of power, and it was Longinus who helped me conduct the affairs of state. True, Odainat prepared me in all military matters, but not in the administration of the kingdom. Affairs of state were run in his absence on campaigns by the second man in the kingdom, Senator Septimius Worôd, who, like Longinus, took refuge at Odainat's court after the Sassanids seized power from the Parthians[8].

The Sassanid takeover disrupted our commercial routes on the eastern bank of the Euphrates and on the Persian Gulf, and necessitated a revision of our relations with Persia. Parthia had great influence on Palmyra – our way of life, dress, art and architecture were partly Parthian – and our relationship was satisfactory. We acted as a barrier between them and the Romans, and the Parthians facilitated the passage of our caravans. There was always a strong pro-Parthian party in Palmyra and it was in the order of things that Worôd, a noble Parthian, should have taken refuge at Odainat's court. He was a man of all seasons, and so appreciated by Odainat that the later gradually turned to him for the most important functions of state, instead of choosing officials from the old merchant aristocracy, for Worôd had an objectivity and a clear view of politics which they lacked. Odainat gave him the *gentilice* 'Septimius', with which only the family and a chosen few were endowed. Worôd excelled in whatever office he was given.

---

8. 'Alī, 1968–73, 101; Will, 1992, 180–1.

His *cursus honorium,* engraved on the console of one of the colonnades, lists his six titles, for he was in turn *procurator ducenarius, juridicus, strategos, agoranome, argabet,* and, above all, *symposiarch*[9] (AD 266) – the highest religious function. Moreover, he was a caravan leader and, as such, he financed and brought back caravans at his expense[10]. He was also chief of troops in Palmyra[11].

Odainat was at his zenith, and power was concentrated in his hands and those of Worôd. The power of the old aristocracy was completely ruined. Odainat was both king and dux, his functions covered the entire Orient, and Worôd held the main administrative functions[12].

The sudden death of Odainat in Emesa left the kingdom and the whole of the Orient in a precarious state. A member of the family, the traitor Maeonius, through whom the Romans had committed their crime, hoped to assume the throne with Roman backing, and the aristocracy was stirring to recover the power it had lost to Odainat. Worôd, the only person capable of implementing administrative continuity in the kingdom, suddenly disappeared from public life. Speculations were rampant, whether it was from despair at losing Odainat, because Worôd was resented as a foreign refugee and could not continue without the protection of Odainat, or because he could not bear to serve

---

9. Seyrig, 1963, 167; 'Alī, 1968–73, 101; Gawlikowski, 1985b, 60; Stoneman, 1992, 79; Will, 1992, 180–1.
10. Mommsen, 1985, 800, n. 1; Sartre-Fauriat, 1997, 258.
11. Février, 1931, 91 and 97.
12. Février, 1931, 100.

under me. He never did serve under me[13]. Worôd was an enigma whom I could never understand, and when I questioned my husband about him, he told me sternly: 'Al-Zabbā', you have your refugee Longinus, and I have mine, Worôd. Stick to the domain of the mind and spirit with your Sophists, and leave the affairs of state to me and Worôd.' It was believed that he returned to Mesopotamia to serve under Sapor.

The assassination of Odainat caused a power vacuum. His son from his first wife, Herodian, who was his heir, and to whom Odainat had given imperial power and titles, was murdered with him. I detested Herodian; he was effeminate, ostentatious and gave himself completely to the luxury of both the Orient and Greece. His tents were embroidered and his pavilions were in silk brocade in the Persian style, but his father indulged him and gave him royal concubines, money and jewels. I hated him, and the more I showed my disgust, the more Odainat increased his indulgence and solicitude, and told me harshly not to be a wicked stepmother[14]. The pretender-traitor Maeonius was ready to usurp the throne, and my enemies spread the rumour that I was in league with him and that I was implicated in my husband's death because of jealousy of my stepson[15] for I wanted to promote Wahaballât, my own son. That I detested my stepson because of his abject and dissolute way of life was public knowledge, but that I would go to the

---

13. Stoneman, 1992, 117.
14. *Hist. Aug., Tyr. Trig.,* 16, 1–3.
15. *Hist. Aug., Tyr. Trig.,* 17, 2.

lengths of scheming to murder him and my husband, shows how contemptible and despicable my enemies could be.

I had to take the reins in my hands, and the first step was to order the death of Maeonius, who was assassinated by the army in Emesa. The second was to proclaim my son Wahaballât (still a minor), King of Kings, and to assume the regency.

The Romans refused to acknowledge Wahaballât's hegemony over the Orient, his father's heritage, and claimed that the powers given to Odainat over all the Orient had been personal honours.

I had to establish my authority as queen and regent for my son by force in order to obtain the reconnaissance of Rome[16]. Longinus, my generals and other advisors from my circle, were by my side to help me navigate in troubled waters, but whatever obstacles or contraries clouded my day, my evenings with my magic circle were enchanted. I indulged myself and my friends. I banqueted with them in the Parthian manner and every item of luxury and refinement that the caravans carried from Babylon, Charactane, India and China, and along the Persian Gulf, the Tigris and the Euphrates, ended at the banqueting table. We sat on tapestries and silk-embroidered cushions in the Parthian fashion; incense and perfumes, delicacies and wines appeared from all corners of the world, and my nightly banquets catered to the senses of sight and smell and the palate, an all-round pleasure, and when the desert sky became diaphanous, Longinus revealed to us the beauties of

---

16. Will, 1992, 181.

Homer and Plato. More than once did I ask him to read selections from his recent commentaries on Plato's *Timaeus*. At times, when some were full of sleep he would discourse on one of his favourite themes, the demiurge or creator as the emanation of the universal mind[17]. He fascinated me with tales about his days as the head of the Academy in Athens, when he marked the birth of Plato by an intellectual dinner party and had as guest the Sophist Nicagoras, who, as Ambassador of Athens to Rome, had written an encomium praising Philip the Arab, and had been the herald of the temple of Eleusis. Besides Apollônios the Grammarian, Demetrios the Geometrician, Prosenes the Peripatetician and Callietes the Stoic, the other Sophists whom Longinus invited, were Hellenised intellectuals from Syria and Arabia[18]: Maior from Arabia, Aspines from Gadara and Porphyry of Tyre, the pupil of Longinus and friend of Plotinus. Night after night, Longinus imbued me with the Platonist mirage of transforming Palmyra into a Utopia, and ideal state[19]. Furthermore, the presence of the Sophists at my court gave an impetus to Neoplatonism – a school of thought shaped by Hellenised Oriental scholars – in the entire region. Longinus and I encouraged Aemilius, a disciple of Plotinus to establish a Neoplatonic school in Apamea[20]. I provided the funds, and Longinus his blessing. Panhellenism was the driving force behind Longinus who

---

17. Stoneman, 1992, 130 and 131.
18. Millar, 1969, 16; Loriot and Nony, 1997, 253.
19. Février, 1931, 106; Sartre-Fauriat, 1997, 273.
20. Shahîd, 1964a, 41, n. 3.

was its most ardent champion at court, surrounding himself with others of the same frame of mind and creed. From the very beginning of my struggle with the Romans I saw the potential of such a movement. Our time was one of tension, of divorce between the Orient and the West, a difference in the way of life, language and culture which increased with the advent of the Pannonian emperors, Claudius and now Aurelian, who championed a Latinised West versus Orient attached to the values of Greek culture, and who now threatened the supporters of Panhellenism[21].

Longinus opened my eyes to the fact that Hellenism was the unifying force in the empire which I was building, based on an Orient under Odainat's control, and which I was now trying to reconquer. Syria, whose urban environment was Hellenised, Egypt with Alexandria as the metropolis of Hellenism, Asia Minor which was Hellenised in depth – all these countries had maintained the heritage of Alexander, and their common language was Greek[22].

My detractors – and they were legion – said maliciously that I consorted with the Neoplatonists, not for the love of philosophy or literature, but for politics and propaganda, in order to reach through them the Hellenised Oriental provinces, to arouse their claim to a Hellenistic Orient and to fan the supremacy of Hellenic culture. The claim was only partly true, for the highlight of my life was to gather in my court the most luminous collection of Greek intellectuals of the age, and the joy that the contact with such intellects

21. Sirinelli, 1995, 428–9.
22. Will, 1992, 203–4; Sirinelli, 1995, 429–30.

gave me cannot be measured. My circle was brilliant, unique and unrivalled, not even by the court of Julia Domna a century ago, but it is true that with their help I seized the cultural, as well as the political initiative[23]. The magic circle of the evenings acted as a polyglot bureau during the day, where I was tutored in Hellenistic history[24] and in the Egyptian language.[25] The propagandists spread the rumour that I was a descendant of the Lagides, and, with the aim of winning Alexandria to my cause, called me the new Cleopatra[26]. Gallinicus, from Petra, schooled me in Egyptian history and offered me a *History of Alexandria* when I became queen of Egypt[27]. Another member of my circle was also from Petra, Genethius, author of a treatise on speech[28]. Aemilius of Apamea was a regular visitor, and Nicomachus of Trebizond, author of a history entitled *From Philip the Arab to Odainat* which focused on the victories of Odainat,[29] was a frequent guest. Cassius Longinus, the leader and guiding light of my circle, was a permanent resident at court, for he loved the climate of Palmyra[30].

Palmyra's increasingly anti-Roman bent and the inevitable forthcoming struggle attracted those who were also struggling against Rome, the Armenians who supported

---

23. Bowersock, 1983, 136.
24. Gagé, 1964, 347.
25. *Hist. Aug., Tyr. Trig.*, 30, 20.
26. *Historia Augusta, Divus Claudius*, 1.1.
27. Bowersock, 1983, 18; Sirinelli, 1995, 430.
28. Millar, 1969, 18; Stoneman, 1992, 132.
29. 'Alī, 1968–73, 108.
30. Commentary by Paschoud, 1996b, 153 on *Hist. Aug., Aurel.*

us in the war with Aurelian, and the Blemmyes, who were ferociously anti-Roman on the southern frontier of Egypt[31]. It is true that I shared with my Sophists and advisors an anti-Roman feeling. They used the military and financial might of Palmyra for their cause and I used them for recruitment and propaganda. The objective was the same – to get rid of Rome.

My circle, however, was not limited to Greek philosophers and rhetors. Christian theologians were welcomed at my court at a time when Christians were periodically persecuted by Rome, notably Paul of Samosata the capital of Commagene who, with my support, obtained the bishopric of Antioch. He in turn helped me win over the Judaeo-Christian centres and the Christian population[32]. Paul of Samosata's help was not limited to attracting the growing Christian population to Palmyra's support, for he was well placed as a native of Samosata to attract a much more important group, the native Syrian population. All Syrian towns, Emesa, Laodicaea, Apamea, and the whole countryside included a strong native component which did not speak Greek, being the Aramaic-speaking descendants of the ancient Aramaeans, Canaanites, and Phoenicians. The Syrians on the whole resented Roman control, and hoped to fare better under a Semitic/Arab Palmyran empire.

Since my Greek intellectuals catered the Hellenic element in the East, and Paul of Samosata and his friends for

---

31. *Hist. Aug., Aurel.*, 28, 2; Starcky, 1960, 1098; Kotula, 1997, 111.
32. Février, 1931, 106; Shahîd, 1984a, 41, n. 3.

the native Syrian, the Arab element in the towns and the desert was left to me.

Paul was a controversial figure. His theology was known to be more Jewish than Christian[33] and was known as the Judaising heresy of Paul[34]. Rumours were spread that he had converted me to Judaism, towards which I never inclined[35]. Another version was that he had converted me to Christianity, while I was only tolerant of Christians and Jews in Palmyra, following in the footsteps of Odainat. In Egypt I was supposed to have converted to Manicheism[36].

Such rumours and gossip were the price that I had to pay for keeping an open mind and inviting to my court the proponents of new, bold, intellectual and theological ideas, for to me each movement had its merits.

To Bishop Paul of Samosata, besides his ecclesiastical functions, I gave the political and secular role of *procurator ducenarius*, together with a high salary of two hundred thousand *sestercii* which made him a very influential man[37] and the leading figure in the city, as well as the representative of the Palmyran regime. At times I called upon him to act as my financial counsellor. I enjoyed the company of the bishop, for he was an open-minded man who had the courage to declare his beliefs, which outraged the Christian clerics in Antioch and gave pleasure to my

---

33. Starcky, 1960, 1098; Kotula, 1997, 110.
34. Sartre-Fauriat, 1997, 273.
35. Starcky, 1960, 1098.
36. Will, 1992, 202.
37. Millar, 1996, 169; Stoneman, 1992, 149.

Neoplatonists. Besides, he represented the Semitic[38] rather than the Graeco-Roman membership of my circle. I never let Paul of Samosata down, for his strong allegiance to Palmyra and his anti-Roman bias had earned him so many enemies. When the ecclesiastical council of Antioch condemned him in 268 and deposed him from office, I encouraged him to hold on to it and not to pay heed to the synod, for I considered him my viceroy in Antioch. He was accused of upholding the belief that Christ's nature was solely human, in defiance of the teaching of the Church.

Four years after the first Council had deposed him, another Council was held in Antioch attended by ecclesiastical representatives from Bostra, Cappadocia, Caesarea and Jerusalem in order to discuss his teaching. Paul attempted to camouflage his heterodox ideas, but to no avail[39]. The Council condemned him and excommunicated him from the Church. A letter was also drafted to the Bishops of Rome and Alexandria, accusing Paul of amassing wealth, of regarding religion as a way of making money, of nurturing the ambition to be a *ducenarius* rather than a bishop, of swaggering in the city squares with a large bodyguard, of sitting on a dais and lofty throne in imitation of the rulers of the world, of slapping his thigh and stamping on the dais surrounded by a badly behaved audience of male and female followers. The letter also claimed that he organised women to sing hymns for him alone in the middle of the church on the great Easter

---

38. Downey, 1961, 264.
39. Eusebius, *Historia Ecclesiastica*, 7, 27.

festival. He refused to adhere to the dogma that the son of God came down from heaven. As to his young and pretty 'spiritual brides', as the Antiochenes called them, and whom he took around with him, he kept them under his roof in order to conceal their incurable sins. The letter ended with his excommunication and the appointment of another bishop in his place, Domnus, the son of his predecessor on the episcopal throne[40]. Paul refused to hand over the church building, relying on me for support. He stayed stubbornly behind in Antioch when we retreated after the battle of Immae. Aurelian on entering the city sided with Paul's adversaries, and Paul was thrown out of the church with utmost indignity by the secular authority[41]. Aurelian's action smacked of revenge against a loyal partisan of Palmyra and a man who embodied Syrian resentment of Rome. His heterodoxy was elaborately exaggerated by the enemies of Palmyra and the friends of Rome, and the gossip about his private life was distorted and enlarged. Alone of my circle, Paul of Samosata escaped execution by Aurelian, for he disappeared from Antioch. The others were accused of anti-Roman activities of helping me recruit partisans in the urban centres and developing contacts with my allies, the Armenians and the Blemmyes on the southern border of Egypt.

Among my counsellors, Paul was a man of outstanding courage and conviction, influential among his Christian parishioners who could not forget the persecution of the

---

40. Euseb., *Hist. Eccl.*, 7, 28-30.
41. Downey, 1961, 265; *Hist. Aug., Aurel.*, 24, 2–6.

Romans under Decius, only twenty years previously. Prospering under Palmyran rule, the Christians and other sects enjoyed tolerance and justice, but when it appealed to Aurelian to depose Paul of Samosata the Church conveniently forgot Rome's frequent persecutions. I often wonder at the Christians' narrow self-righteousness, opportunism and lack of dignity.

I have been trying to shirk the painful subject of which, even as a shade, I cannot come to terms with – Aurelian's mass execution of all my advisors, counsellors, Sophists, and generals, of all those whom I trusted and loved and on whose devotion and hard work the Palmyran Empire was built. How can I speak of the assassination of Longinus in cold blood? My defeat and captivity, and the destruction of Palmyra were not enough for Aurelian, that bloodthirsty barbarian. He had found my Achilles heel, Longinus, and he wounded me by murdering him.

I was kept in the dark for a few days after my capture on the Euphrates. Palmyra surrendered and Aurelian carried with him to Emesa all my counsellors, as well as thousands of Palmyrans who had fought till the end. I was not allowed to see any of them, neither Longinus, nor my generals, Zabadas and Zabbaï. One day the slave who brought my food was silently sobbing and when I asked the reason she said that early that morning Aurelian had executed all my advisors. 'And Longinus?', I asked. 'Yes, the old philosopher was the last to die.' Silence – a long silence. I stood without moving, without uttering a cry, until a tribune sent by Aurelian entered my room and said: 'The emperor has held a tribunal and told your advisors that their Queen Zenobia had exonerated herself by putting the blame of revolting against Rome on them and that they had taken advantage of her being a woman to mislead her[42]. For that reason, he has executed them and reprieved you. He was especially hard on Longinus.'

I could not speak. How could he tell such elaborate falsehoods[43], such preposterous lies, that I accused Longinus of inciting me against Rome? Rome was never my master to revolt against. My son, Wahaballât, *Imperator* and *Augustus*, and I the *Augusta*, ruled by right the eastern half of the Roman Empire, inherited from my husband who had saved it from the Persians. How far could Aurelian take lies and calumny to tarnish my integrity and reputation?

This severe, savage and bloody prince[44], the emperor of the Romans, is not only a crude barbarian but a liar! I wanted to shout, but who could hear me in my prison cell? How dare he accuse me of saving my skin at the expense of my friends[45]? I wanted to cry that he hates all things of the mind and that is why he killed the most brilliant mind of the age.

He executed Longinus the Sublime, because he had a score to settle with him, firstly his Panhellenism, and secondly in order to cover up his own suspect role in the murder of Emperor Gallienus, a friend of philosophers[46] and

---

42. Zos., *Hist. Nov.*, 1, 56, 2–3; Stoneman, 1992, 131.
43. Will, 1992, 203.
44. *Hist. Aug., Aurel.*, 36, 2.
45. Homo, 1904, 108; Février, 1931, 106; Stoneman, 1992, 131.
46. Will, 1992, 203.

a man who spoke Greek, an emperor resented and hated by a number of senators and army officers, amongst whom was Aurelian.

He hated Longinus the Sublime with a vehemence that only a barbarian and a stranger to Greek culture could harbour; a man whom Apollonius of Tyana, philosopher and friend of the gods appearing to him in a vision during the siege of Tyana, had to address in Latin to make himself understood, for this Pannonian emperor was a man who could not speak Greek[47]!

Aurelian executed Longinus, one of the last Greek intellectuals, a Sophist, known and admired all over the world, and put the blame on me. But to complete the horror, Aurelian had the bad taste to think that I should be grateful for my life, while the only reason he had saved me was for me to be the chief attraction in his Triumph. His cruelty and thirst for blood impaired his reasoning, for how could I want to save my life by betraying my friends, when I had already decided on extinction at the very moment of my defeat and captivity? I had lost all, I had nothing to save, least of all my life!

I faced so many calumnies in my life, but this attack on my integrity, on my honour was the last straw, for how could anybody believe the preposterous lie?

Aurelian well knew that Julia Aurelia Septimia, the queen of the Orient, does not betray her friends[48]. He executed Longinus the champion of Hellenism because he

---

47. *Hist. Aug., Aurel.,* 24.
48. 'Alī, 1968–73, 124, cites S. Ritzval, in *Al-Mashriq*, no. 22, p. 1059.

had proved that the Hellenic Renaissance was not dead. That was the cold vengeance of a man who was truly completely estranged from Greek culture[49].

Longinus, sublime in death as he was in life, faced death with courage and bestowed comfort on his afflicted friends[50]. He followed the executioner without uttering a complaint, pitying me who remained alive. His death was reminiscent of and on the same level as that of his master, Socrates[51].

How could Aurelian's crude and vulgar mind ever fathom my relationship with Longinus? His memory haunts me and plagues my shade. I can hear him still talking of Plato, deep into the night, when the light of the candles was blown by the light breeze, and the sound of a flute came from the farthest corner of the palace, and the face of the moon over the temple of Bêl was covered by a cloud. I still hear his voice fading beyond the funeral towers that rose from the darkness, and were shimmering in the desert night, reminding us that all was ephemeral and fleeting.

49. Sirinelli, 1995, 429–30.
50. *Hist. Aug., Aurel.,* 30, 2–3; Zos., *Hist. Nov.,* 56, 3.
51. Hitti, 1951, 444.

Explanatory Note:

Zenobia Vilified

Some modern historians have rejected the version of Zenobia's betrayal of her friends[1], while others have accepted the validity of the version of her betrayal to save her own skin, and have been even more vehement in their vilification and condemnation than the Classical writers. Février describes her as ferociously ambitious, a small, thin woman with pursed lips, devoured by an insatiable lust for power, so that when she lost all, she broke down[2]. This queen conducted herself with cowardice, and in a most repugnant manner, for all she could think of was to save her life by accusing her friends. Trembling in front of the soldiers who were demanding her head, she charged others, and Aurelian executed them all[3].

Gibbon had already painted the same picture: 'as female fortitude is commonly artificial, the courage of Zenobia deserted her in the hour of trial, and ignominiously purchased life by the sacrifice of her fame and her friends.'[4]

According to Stoneman, Longinus was vilified as the architect of the queen's ambition, even by the queen herself who saved her skin by blaming her advisors[5]. Likewise,

---

1.   Will, 1992; Sirinelli, 1995.
2.   Février, 1931, 104.
3.   Février, 1931, 136.
4.   Watson, 1998, 87.
5.   Stoneman, 1992, 131.

Cisek asserts that Zenobia tried to accuse her counsellors, especially Longinus[6].

These examples of vilification are linked perhaps to the image of the Oriental, revelling in pomp, finery and luxury, effeminate, weak of character and faithless. Zenobia has constantly been associated with or measured against these blemishes[7]. Her husband, Odainat, has been described as one who, like all Arabs, loved luxury, but at the same time made use of sudden brutal physical energy[8].

In fact, Zenobia's suicide proves that she did not have to accuse and blame her friends in order to save her life.

---

6. Cisek, 1994, 113.
7. Watson, 1998, 87.
8. Février, 1931, 79.

CHAPTER III

An Arab Empire

I once had a dream, a distant mirage that hovered over my nights and days, and for that dream I put aside the age-long Palmyran prudence and the fragile diplomatic skill with which Palmyra joggled and manoeuvred between the two great powers for the sake of its commerce[1]. I dreamed of an Arab Empire, and for that dream I took a calculated risk. I challenged Rome, and for a moment in time it was given to me to fulfil my dream (Fig. 11). I built an Arab empire and aimed to crown it by adding Rome itself, but then the calculation misfired – not through my weakness, but through the universal law of fate – and the price was the destruction of six centuries of brilliant existence of the dwelling place of the gods and the home of all men, the beloved city that was once Palmyra.

My plan for an Arab empire was to be realised, in its first phase, as a united Panhellenic Orient, independent and detached from Rome, this entailing the reconquest of Odainat's dominions, for his elimination had resulted in unsettled conditions in the frontier zone, had brought havoc to our commerce and permitted encroachment on our

---

1. Dussaud, 1955, 76.

territory by our deadly enemies, the federation of the Tanūkh whom I was compelled to crush once and for all.

A Panhellenic Orient, independent of Rome, was not a new idea. Such a secession had already taken place during the triumvirate when Mark Anthony had ruled the eastern half of the Roman Empire. In a second phase, the aim was to restore Arab domination over central government[2]. The rise to imperial dignity was not new to the Arabs; it had started with the Severan dynasty with whom we had strong links. The family adopted the *gentilice* of Septimius Severus in gratitude for his making my husband's grandfather a Roman senator. The Empress Julia Domna, from neighbouring Emesa, who had ruled the empire while her son Caracalla was perpetually campaigning with his army, as well as her two nephew emperors, and her sister Julia Maesa, her nieces Julia Soaemias and Julia Mammaea, had all showered favours on Palmyra. Another neighbour, a member of a Safaitic tribe in the Hawran, the Emperor Philip the Arab, had made my husband a Roman senator[3].

I was eight years old when Philip the Arab was assassinated, but I remember that he was mourned in the family as one of our own. The impact of his death was tremendous; it plunged the whole area in gloom, but only fifteen years ago, two years before I got married, another Arab, Uranius Antoninus, a Sampsigeramus from Julia's family and a priest of the sun, claimed the *imperium*, repelled the Persians from Emesa, and restored the Arabs to

---

2.   Dussaud, 1955, 161–3; Stoneman, 1992, 161 and 163.
3.   Zahran, 2001, 36 and 70.

central government just before Odainat took upon himself the task of protecting the empire.

There was a great difference, however, between me and my Arab predecessors, for they ruled the establishment as Romans, fought Roman wars, and their military operations were conducted from Rome, but I ran the war from Palmyra, an Arab city, with Arab troops that followed the principles of desert warfare, and as such I aimed at ruling Rome as head of a mighty and wealthy Arab kingdom, with a sea of Arabs behind me, for although I am Hellenised, I am an Arab queen, very conscious of my identity[4].

I was amused when the Romans claimed I was a usurper, with separatist ambitions to detach the East from Rome, for they could not envisage that I wanted to control the whole empire, and that my hold on the Orient was only the foretaste of an Arab Empire. I went so far as to design the chariot in which, victorious, I planned to enter Rome[5]. I had no qualms, for I had not forgotten the price of loyalty to Rome as in the case of Odainat, it meant a treacherous death by assassination, for that is how Rome rewards the faithful.

To put my dream in practice I began with the army, which was separate from the Roman army and had its own system[6].

I retrained and re-equipped the army which had gained invaluable experience in Odainat's wars and in guarding the commercial routes in Anatha, Hīra and Dura, as well as

---

4. Levi Della Vida, 1944, 40; Shahîd, 1984a, 38.
5. *Hist. Aug., Aurel.,* 32, 4.
6. Ingholt, 1976, 124.

other military posts and forts. It was mainly recruited from the Arabian tents of the desert and from Syrian villages, with veterans and disaffected soldiers from Roman legions. The army was my power base, for Palmyra had to become a strong Arab state. In this I followed Odainat's policy of depending on Arab tribes in the desert and the Arab elements in the cities[7].

The first act of Roman hostility began early in my reign. The Emperor Gallienus refused to recognise the rights of my son Wahaballât to his father's domain, which extended from the Taurus to the Euphrates, for he claimed that the powers given to Odainat were personal and not hereditary[8], so I had to assert my authority as queen and regent for my son by force. Gallienus sent immediately Praetorian Prefect Hercalianus with a large army to the East under the pretext of fighting the Persians, but in reality he was sent to fight against Palmyra in order to restore Roman power and to reinstate the Roman legions in my domain, especially in Antioch and the rest of Syria[9].

I went to meet him at the head of my army. He was defeated and killed.

The death of Gallienus in Milan in 268 and the ensuing disorders in the West overshadowed this incident. His successor, elected by the soldiers, Claudius the Goth (268–70) was busy in the Danube. He defeated the Goths of whom he killed fifty thousand and received from the Senate

---

7. 'Alī, 1968–73, 113; Shahîd, 1984a, 151.
8. Will, 1992, 181.
9. Bowersock, 1990, 8.

the title *Gothicus Maximus*. It was during his short reign of two years that I reconquered the Orient but to save appearances, I had his portrait depicted on coins struck in Antioch, as Odainat had done for Gallienus[10].

My domination over Syria and Mesopotamia was tacitly admitted by Rome but I had to force it to recognise my domination over the rest of Odainat's inheritance which legally comprised Egypt, a part of Asia Minor, Cilicia and Upper Cappadocia[11].

Rome watched as the situation in Syria and Arabia grew tense, and waited for the propitious moment to crush the rising menace of Palmyra, but I did not wait until attacked. I immediately went to war and reconquered what was mine by right. I controlled the eastern half and the richest provinces of the empire, but that was not enough. My ambition went much further. I aimed at Rome and made a bid for the whole empire[12].

Carving an Arab Palmyran empire in the reign of Claudius was easy. Firstly I had to ensure the control of Syria and Mesopotamia. I occupied Antioch in 268, the year Claudius came to the throne. There was no resistance in the rest of Syria, as both the Panhellenists and the native Semites rallied to my side, relieved to be rid of the Romans. On the death of Claudius, the mint of Antioch which was one of the largest twenty-two mints operating in the Roman Empire, with its fifteen separate workshops, was suspended.

---

10. *Hist. Aug., Gallieni Duo*, 13,5.
11. Mommsen, 1985, 805.
12. 'Alī, 1968–73, 113; Millar, 1996, 335; Sartre, 2001, 981.

However, I reopened the mint under Palmyran control and issued coins in the joint names of Wahaballât, marking the fourth year of his reign, and of Aurelian, who succeeded Claudius, in the first year of his reign, but this situation did not last[13].

At the head of my army, with Zabadas, the chief commander at my side, I swept through Palestine during the reign of Claudius and crashed through the province of Arabia, which suffered from insecurity and was at the mercy of Beduin threats. In Bostra, the capital of the province, the Legio III Cyrenaica offered stiff resistance, which forced me to destroy the legion's temple of Jupiter Hammon. I sent a detachment to the ancient capital of the province, Petra, and destroyed its temple of Jupiter (Ḳaṣr al-bint)[14]. The Safaitic Arab tribes in the Hawran supported my army[15], as well as other major tribes.

The Tanūkh, who had already infiltrated the province, were now fighting us alongside the Romans. I must confess that my vehemence in the province of Arabia, a fury which I showed nowhere else through all my wars of conquest, was an assault upon the upstart Tanūkh, newcomers to the area, who resented my control over the Arab tribes of Syria and Arabia, and aspired to replace the Palmyrans as lords of the desert.

---

13. Downey, 1961, 265; Stoneman, 1992, 117.
14. Graf, 1989a, 391 cites Zayadine (1983), whose excavations on behalf of the Department of Antiquities of Jordan have uncovered evidence of the destruction of the temple.
15. *Hist. Aug., Aurel.*, 26, 1 and 27, 4–5; Graf, 1989a, 322–3: Safaitic inscriptions show sympathy for Zenobia.

On my passage to Egypt I destroyed Thainata (Umm al-Djimal) in Transjordan, which had become recently a centre of Tanūkh influence[16]. This showdown was to teach them a lesson but they were seething with revenge as they attributed to me the death of their chief Djadhima.

I proceeded to Egypt with an army of seventy thousand to answer the call of a priest of Alexandria, a fellow Arab, Timagenes (Tamdjin)[17], to free Egypt from the Romans, and of Firmus, a rich Alexandrian, who offered to help with money[18]. The conquest of Egypt was easy, almost a voluntary submission, owing to the discontent of the Egyptians, and their exploitation by the Romans for three centuries. We had strong local support in Alexandria[19], but above all the invasion was well prepared, for to the Alexandrians I was the descendant of Cleopatra.

I will not deny that one of the factors of my zeal for the conquest of Egypt was commercial, especially since I struck at the stomach of Rome, for Egypt supplied one third of the Romans' consumption of grain. Palmyran merchants who had been well established in Alexandria for a hundred years before the invasion facilitated our task. Many of them traded in weapons and equipment, but, above all else, the conquest of Egypt meant that the traffic to India was now on the Nile, and its Red Sea prolongation, for, since the

---

16. Bowersock, 1983, 13 and 133; Sartre, 2001, 986.
17. 'Alī, 1968–73, 265.
18. Schwartz, 1976, 19; Mommsen, 1985, 806.
19. *Hist. Aug., Claud.*, 1-2; Zos., *Hist. Nov.*, 1, 44; 1–2; Graf, 1989a, 391; Watson, 1998, 62.

Sassanids had come to power, our commerce on the Lower Euphrates had suffered a progressive slowdown, the northern routes had been almost closed as a result of the destruction of Dura and Ana, and the ships that were loaded with goods to be transported by our caravans were nearly always stopped at the Persian Gulf.

The conquest of Egypt saved our commerce by opening for us the commercial routes which Egypt had with Abyssinia, Arabia, Syria and India, either through Petra, or the Red Sea coast road. In controlling Egypt, we controlled communication between India and the Mediterranean and monopolised commerce with India, which threatened Rome and added to our resources[20]. Coptos on the Nile, where goods transited on their way from Africa to the Orient, was militarily protected, while our archers guarded the land routes[21]. We also ensured security in Upper Egypt, for the Blemmyes, who under the Romans threatened the caravans on their way to the Red Sea, were now our allies[22].

I respected the special status that Egypt had under Rome. It was governed by a viceroy, directly responsible to the emperor, for it was considered his personal property. I therefore appointed Timagenes as my viceroy, and Zabadas entrusted to him a garrison of five thousand Palmyrans, before we turned back home to prepare for the invasion of Asia Minor.

---

20. Février, 1931, 108.
21. Sartre-Fauriat, 1997, 27.
22. Schwartz, 1976, 140–6.

Meanwhile, Probus, the Roman governor of Egypt, who had been absent during the conquest, chasing with the fleet Scythian pirates on the Black Sea[23], returned, gathered an army of pro-Roman Egyptians and attacked Alexandria, slaughtering our garrison. I sent Zabadas back to Egypt and he defeated Probus at Babylon of Egypt (Fustāt, modern Cairo). Arabs in the eastern part of Egypt helped our army, especially around the fort at Babylon[24]. Probus committed suicide[25].

I was now prepared for the conquest of Asia Minor. Our army with generals Zabadas and Zabbaï advanced with hardly any resistance and occupied Ancyra in Galatia[26], but Chalcedon offered stiff resistance and closed its gates. However, our army was facing Byzantium, and the commercial routes of the Bosphorus, whence came wheat, salted fish and slaves, were now under our control. The Gothic invasion had paralysed these routes, but now they were open again for commerce[27].

To the provinces which Odainat had governed, Arabia, Syria, Mesopotamia and Cilica, I now added Asia Minor up to Bithynia in the north and Egypt in the south[28].

I now controlled the richest provinces of the empire, but I had to pay a little price for the Persian alliance by giving

---

23. Schwartz, 1976, 148.
24. 'Alī, 1968–73, 115.
25. Starcky and Gawlikowski, 1985, 62.
26. *Zos., Hist. Nov.*, 1, 50; Will, 1992, 187.
27. Hitti, 1951, 440; 'Alī, 1968–73, 117; Février, 1931, 110.
28. Cisek, 1994, 104.

up some of Odainat's conquests, part of Mesopotamia, Babylon and the city of Charax on the Persian Gulf[29].

But even though I controlled from my Arab city of Palmyra the eastern half of the Roman Empire, my ambition was not appeased. I still lusted after the whole empire but as an equal, for Odainat and I had protected Rome as equals. Or was I less capable than Julia Domna, who had virtually ruled the empire as mother of Caracalla, or than the other Juliae who had wielded equal power over their emperor sons? Odainat had brought down Persia and I could hold my own against Rome. I planned making Palmyra a third power that would dominate both Persia and Rome[30].

Who can give me back those glorious years? When my dream was almost coming true, when the ambassadors, the envoys, even the humblest of my subjects from the Taurus to Sinai were rushing and bowing at my door. They came in groups, or alone, tired, sad or hopeful, they had crossed deserts and seas, to ask Zenobia for justice, for mercy. I could not but make their problems and their dreams my own, and give them at times more than they sought. Longinus was permanently at my shoulder, urging me towards an ideal state – the Utopia, the mirage of the Platonists – raising my spirit if I floundered, pleading for equity, for justice, trying in vain to elevate the simple mortal that I was to unimagined heights. Yes, I revelled in power, especially the power to bring prosperity to the ordinary people of the empire. As to justice, however hard I tried, I

---

29. *Hist. Aug., Aurel.*, 28, 24; Février, 1931, 103 and 106.
30. Stoneman, 1992, 162–3; Millar, 1996, 335; Sartre, 2001, 981.

can never claim to have achieved it, for human justice is so imperfect and so frail – its absoluteness can only be attributed to the gods. I revelled in the fact that for the first time in Roman history, the Oriental part returned to its former state before the conquest of Pompey, when substantial parts of the same area had been in the hands of the Arabs, princes and dynasts. And now, four centuries later, the area had reverted to Arab rule[31].

Rome was flabbergasted, furious, scandalised that a woman, an Arab queen from a desert city could defeat the invincible Roman legions. The Senate started to plead with Emperor Claudius to deliver them from the Palmyrans in a clamour which was shouted five times, and above all to deliver them from Zenobia in a cry repeated seven times[32].

Earlier, Claudius had written to the Senate that he was ashamed that all his archers had deserted to Zenobia[33]. Evidently he had not realised that the archers in the Roman army were Palmyrans!

Claudius was in no position to fight in the East, as he was busy fighting in the West and was obliged to tacitly admit my control of the Orient. He was practical enough to accept a situation beyond his control and to come to an agreement. I recognised a nominal Roman hegemony, while he admitted my domination. The agreement lasted through his two years of office and held for a short while when Aurelian replaced him. What shall I say of Aurelian, the

---

31. Shahîd, 1984a, 151–2.
32. *Hist. Aug., Claud.,* 3, 4.
33. 'Alī, 1968–73, 114.

cruel barbarian who killed the son of his own sister, the man who reintroduced the religion of the sun to Rome, the man with whom I tried to compromise as I ordered the mint of Antioch to strike the coins in his name as *Caesar* and *Augustus*? Admittedly, he was depicted on the reverse, while on the obverse, Wahaballât was termed *Dux Romanorum*. Aurelian accepted the situation temporarily, and, as long as he was fighting the Vandals and the Goths in Danubian lands, we were safe. Meanwhile, my plans were set in motion. Chalcedon and Byzantium had to be conquered before we crossed the Bosphorus into Thrace, and from there we would proceed to Rome.

I was drunk with victory and power, and the illusion lulled me into believing it would last forever. The caravan desert city ruled more than half of the civilised world from the Bosphorus to the Euphrates for five glorious years. My dream of an Arab Empire had come true. My people, like me, were drunk with pride and full of joy, everybody was getting rich, and the rich even richer. They sang on the streets underneath the palace window about my beauty, my courage, and sang ribald songs mocking my Sophists fighting battles of the mind rather than the bed[34].

My days were feverish and full, and although I was preparing for war, I did not neglect the administration. I first received reports from Antioch and Alexandria, the two most important cities which I ruled, and which enjoyed for the first time direct simultaneous administration by the

---

34. Browning, 1979, 9.

Palmyran central power. I then consulted with my military staff, strategists and generals, but I did not neglect the city, for whether we were at peace or at war, our commercial activity had to continue, and we could never forget that trade was our lifeline.

The smooth functioning of the caravan-trade was a priority. I spent much time with the chieftains, who led the caravans to the great warehouses of the Euphrates, to Vologesias, not far from Ctesiphon, to Seleucia on the Tigris, to Phorath and Charax Spasinu, twin cities on the mouth of the river where the Tigris and Euphrates meet[35], and even though the traffic on the Euphrates slowed down considerably with the advent of the Sassanids and became more sporadic, crossing the Euphrates on skin rafts and hiring boats to navigate the Persian Gulf up to the basin of the Indus – a complicated process – continued.

I supervised the collection of money at the outset of the voyage, for food and equipment, for men and animals and payments to the local chiefs and notables through whose territory the caravans passed. The newly opened trade route through the Nile and the Red Sea to India had to be regulated, and new trading routes in Asia Minor had to be explored. Caravans which were actually a tribal enterprise were assisted by our trading posts in almost all the cities which they visited. All precautions had to be taken, since the caravans at times faced real danger[36].

---

35. Mommsen, 1985, 800.
36. Dussaud, 1955, 74, 77; Teixidor, 1984, 46.

The situation in the market was a profusion of colour, crowds and noise, with the desert tribes who came to sell their wool and butter, but the two items that I had to continually regulate with the Senate were the salt monopoly and the traffic of slaves, who were often captured pirates, war prisoners or free men heavily in debt. These two items provided a particularly large profit to the state treasury[37].

The rural hinterland was a major worry, for the problem of irrigation in an arid zone necessitated the building of a dam, eighteen metres high and two hundred metres long, which stored sufficient water and cost the city a large amount of money, but enabled us to create a pastoral economy in the mountain villages around Palmyra, for a great part of our population was semi-nomadic and practised stock farming[38]. The rest of the day was spent in the town council (*Boule*) supervising and regulating the collection of taxes.

With what joy, after such days, I looked forward to evenings with my Sophists, when the nights enveloped us in a diaphanous desert mist, and nectar was served by the silent eunuchs, beardless, long-haired, effeminate youths, so often portrayed behind their dead masters in our funerary sculptures[39].

Our discussions took a new turn with the new territories added to the kingdom, now an empire, but I dismissed the talk of war and conquest, wealth and power, and told them they were meaningless without music and without poetry. I

---

37. Teixidor, 1984, 78, 82–3.
38. Teixidor, 1984, 71 and 73.
39. Stoneman, 1992, 122.

harassed them with my tortured questions on existence, on the ephemeral nature of things, on the universal law of fate, and they in turn teased and mocked me saying they did not know whether to address the Roman empress, the Arab queen or just Zenobia, and I told them, laughing, that the dichotomy was possible only because of their Hellenism.

This beautiful life was brief. Lament no more, Zenobia, for such are these things. I recall the five glorious years before the advent of Aurelian, the fierce barbarian of whom I now received reports from our pani-stricken agents indicating that he was back in Rome. I feared the worst, and, although on his accession to the throne I respected the agreement I had with Claudius and thus I kept his portrait on the coins struck in Antioch and Alexandria, he could not forgive the blow to his pride. That he, an emperor, should be depicted on the reverse of coins earned me his everlasting grudge[40].

Back in Rome he won over the opposition of the Senate and was free to attack us, especially since with the death of Sapor he shrewdly concluded that I could not count on Persian support[41]. Since his first step was the reconquest of Asia Minor, he also tried hard to weaken the Hellenistic support for Palmyra, which was extremely strong in Greek cities. I also knew that he had fifteen legions, including the twelve fierce Danubian legions, the praetorian guard and two hundred thousand soldiers[42].

---

40. Mommsen, 1985, 806.
41. Février, 1931, 117–8.
42. Cisek, 1994, 105.

Aurelian was intent on a rapid reconquest of Egypt, because Rome could not do long without Egyptian wheat, and, was sending Probus[43], his best general, for the campaign. For us, the problem was that we had pulled most of our garrison out of Egypt for the conquest of Asia Minor.

I struck back, glad to renounce any sham pretence of Roman hegemony. In AD 271, I cancelled the agreement made with Claudius and erased the portrait of Aurelian from the coinage. Wahaballât figured alone on both coins of Antioch and Alexandria with the legend *Augustus*. I was *Augusta Sebaste*, empress and queen, in inscriptions and on milestones. On the reverse of my coins was depicted Selene, the moon goddess, as on the coins of my idol Julia Domna. I gave Wahaballât all the titles of a Roman emperor *Persicus Maximus, Arabicus Maximus, Adiabenicus Maximus, Pius, Felix, Invictus, Augustus*[44].

I ordered all milestones on the Nova Trajana in Transjordan from Bostra to Philadelphia and on the road to Emesa and Byblos, as well as on other roads in my kingdom to be inscribed: 'For the salvation and victory of Septimius Wahaballâtus Athenadorus, the very illustrious king and Corrector of the Orient, son of Septimius Odainat, King of Kings and for the salvation of Septimia Betzabbai, very illustrious queen, mother of the King of Kings, daughter of Antiochus.'[45]

---

43. The future emperor and the namesake of the former governor of Egypt.
44. Stoneman, 1992, 123 and 171; Kotula, 1997, 116; Sartre-Fauriat, 1997, 269.
45. Will, 1992, 187; Kotula, 1997, 116.

This was a declaration of war on my part. I defied Aurelian and wounded his pride, and my bid for empire took a dangerous turn for the Romans. Aurelian could not stomach sharing the title of *Augustus*, for he felt that he alone should bear it as well as the radiating crown which made him the earthly image of a supreme god[46].

Aurelian, the barbarian, stood between me and my dream of an Arab Empire that included Rome, and so, disregarding caution and omens, I decided to fight him with all my might.

---

46. Février, 1931, 115.

Explanatory Note:

The Arabs and Palmyra

Palmyra was an Arab kingdom with a predominantly Arab population. To the Arab historians, these were Arabs who spoke Arabic, most probably a north Arabian dialect[1], but as in many towns in Syria, the population of Palmyra included an Aramaean component. Nevertheless, the Arab character of Palmyra and the ambition of Zenobia to make of her desert kingdom an Arab Empire have been put into question by a few, modern, eminent and reputed Western historians, who have qualified Palmyran civilization vaguely as 'ethnic', 'Oriental', 'Semitic', 'Aramaean' or 'Syrian', but never 'Arab'. Teixidor states categorically: 'Palmyra was an Aramaean city – and it is a mistake to consider it as an Arab town.' He described the ruling family of Odainat as 'princely of Aramaean origin', and considers 'the ascension of Odainat' to have been a triumph for the Aramaeans of Syria and for their language.'[2]

According to Will, the idea that Palmyra may have been an 'Arab kingdom' derived from the modern discovery of the Arab world, which was triggered in France by R. Dussaud's book *La pénétration des Arabes en Syrie avant l'Islam* (1955). In Will's view, it was hardly possible to qualify Palmyra as an Arab town. He even wondered

---

1. Al-Bounni, 1978, 91 (quoted by Halak, 2002, 34–5); Shahîd, 1984a, 146.
2. Teixidor, 1993, 713, 723 and 725.

85

whether Zenobia had ever wished for an ethnic and cultural Semitic East, both anti-Greece and anti-Rome, and concluded that she did not. To prove his point, he put forward the fact that nobody in Palmyra boasted of their Arab origin. Another proof was that a few Safaitic inscriptions have been found in Palmyra (ten out of ninety-three)[3]. But why should there be Safaitic inscriptions in Palmyra? The Safaitic tribes of the Hawran spoke an Arabic dialect derived from southern Arabic and carved their inscriptions on rocks, while Palmyrans spoke Arabic and Aramaic, their inscriptions being written in Aramaic, the official language. As to Palmyrans boasting of their origin, it appears that Will was not aware of the genealogy of Odainat and Zenobia detailed in the Arabic historical sources[4].

Février has contested that the masses in Palmyra were Arab[5], and has described Zenobia's ambition as a fit of madness ('*coup de folie*'), wondering whether she really believed that Wahaballât could replace Elagabalus[6].

Sartre does not believe in Zenobia's struggle for an Arab empire and considers that nothing allows us to interpret her secession from the Roman Empire as foreshadowing the rise of a political movement against an occupying force, with the aim of creating an Arab empire. The conquest of Egypt and

---

3. Will, 1992, 177 and 199–201.
4. Al-Iṣfahānī, *Kitāb al-Aghānī*, Vol. 15, 252; Ibn Khaldūn, *Ta'rikh*, Vol. 2, 261.
5. Février, 1932, 219.
6. Février, 1931, 117.

Asia Minor shows that the goal was not a 'Syrian' Empire (and even less so an 'Arab empire'). He argues, moreover, that Athenadoros, the Hellenised name of Wahaballât, represents a contradiction to an ethnic claim[7]. Sartre's interpretation of Zenobia's wars includes at least the recognition of the possibility that Zenobia aimed at creating an Arab Empire. As to Wahaballât's Greek name, it is well known that the upper echelons of the population of Syria had been thoroughly Hellenised, and, as such, many Arabs gave themselves a Greek name, which was usually the translation into Greek of their Arabic name: Athenadoros is a literal translation of Wahaballât ('gift of Allât'), Allât being assimilated in Palmyra with Athena.

Fergus Millar contends that there is no evidence suggesting that the Palmyrans, whom we tend to see as sedentarised Arabs, saw themselves as Arabs, or that contemporary outsiders saw them as such. He recognises however, Zenobia's Arab ambition, for he states that the 'brief claim by a "queen" and her son from Palmyra did represent the abortive assertion of an "Arab" or "Syrian" nationalism, based on a city where social and cultural history was unlike that of any other provincial community in the empire.'[8] In fact, Arab dynasties of Syria and Mesopotamia called themselves Edessans, Hatrans, Emesans, Nabateans, Itureans, and not Arabs. The Palmyran rulers were no exception.[9]

---

7. Sartre, 2001, 981–2.
8. Millar, 1996, 331–4.
9. Kaizer, 2002, 40 and 57–8.

The litany of persisting denials of Zenobia's aspirations for an Arab Empire continues in T. Kaizer's recent work, as he asserts: 'Apart from anachronistic presuppositions, there are certainly no grounds for viewing the events as a pre-Islamic pan-Arab movement against the Western world.' Kaizer further argues against the notion of 'Arabness' when Wahaballât received the imperial victory titles: *Persicus Maximus, Arabicus Maximus, Adiabenicus Maximus*, forgetting that he received those titles from Zenobia who aspired to the imperial throne, and that another Arab, Philip, had borne these titles before.

A rival school of eminent Western and Arab historians, however, emphasises the Arab character of Palmyra. In the third century, Palmyra was an Arab principality with a dynasty, the family of Odainat, which had been at the head of the city since post-Severan turmoils[10]. In Dussaud's opinion, it is wrong to treat the Palmyrans as a separate and non- Arab race simply because they spoke Aramaic, for Aramaic was not only spoken by Arabs in Palmyra, but also by the Arabs of Nabatea, Emesa, Iturea, Hatra and Edessa[11]. Hitti asserts that (in spite of their writing in Aramaic), the majority of Palmyra's people were Arabs[12]. According to Van Berchem, the names of tribes inscribed on tesserae in Palmyra, indicate clans and families also found in the inscriptions of other Arab groups. The four tribes which in Palmyra formed the civic corps were predominantly

---

10. Gawlikowski, 1985a, 251.
11. Dussaud, 1955, 77.
12. Hitti, 1951, 443.

traditional Arab tribes, each with its own sanctuary and religious pantheon[13].

Of the Arab tribes which entered Syria and 'Iraq in the Hellenistic period and founded dynasties in Emesa, Edessa, Characne, Iturea, Nabatea and Palmyra, the Arab element was strongest in Palmyra, in the opinion of G. Levi Della Vida. The Palmyrans were Aramised and Hellenised Arabs, but to a higher degree than the Nabateans: the personal names and tribal organisations of the Palmyrans betray their Arab origins. This is confirmed by A. Shahîd who views the Palmyrans, although subjected to foreign influences more than the Nabateans had been, as remaining Arab in ethos, mores and religious practices. The Arab character of Palmyra was also stronger than that of Emesa under the Severii[14].

Most Palmyrans were Arabs. The name *Tadmur* derives etymologically according to Arabic lexicons from the verb *damara* ('to destroy')[15]. Safaitic *dmr* is 'to protect'. Thus, *Tadmur* means the 'city of protection', a shelter or a refuge for the people of the desert.

Aramaic and Arabic were spoken in Palmyra, Greek by intellectuals and Latin by some. Palmyran inscriptions contain many Arabic words. The influence of Arabic was considerable, mainly in the sphere of religion and personal names, and there are many Arabic loan words. Palmyran

---

13. Van Berchem, 170–3.
14. Levi Della Vida, 1944, 40.
15. Maraqten, 1995, 91.

was also influenced by Akkadian and Greek[16].

In sum, more attention should be paid to the Arabic tradition as regards the Arab pedigree of Odainat and Zenobia and the very Arab environment of Tadmur. Palmyra had a strong Arab identity and consciousness of its power to endow the Palmyran dynasty with the *imperium*[17]. Zenobia embodied those traits and achieved precisely that aim.

16. Maraqten, 1995, 92 and 105.
17. Shahîd, 1984a, 38.

CHAPTER IV

The Ruse of Zabadas

Who would have guessed that I, Zenobia, whom the world took for serious, stubborn, disciplined, severe and erudite, had her frivolous, weird and bizarre side. Truly I did, and I enjoyed it, for in all the disasters that have befallen me it was my erratic character that saved me. I laughed about myself and everything else, – above all, Aurelian – yes, he won the war, but I had the last laugh!

I did not have to have a pretext to break finally from Rome. All those compromises during the reigns of Gallienus, Claudius, and even at the onset of Aurelian's accession had exhausted me. However, Aurelian saw the writing on the wall, when I ordered the mints of Antioch and Alexandria to remove his effigy. The Latin coins, the *Antonini*, proclaimed Wahaballât Roman Emperor. The diadem on his bust disappeared and was replaced by the radiating crown and the *paludamentum*. The legend stated: *Imperator Caesar, Wahaballâtus Augustus*, and on the reverse the traditional Roman legend *Aeternitas Augustus*.

On some coins struck in Antioch, my legend was on the obverse, *Septimia Zenobia Augusta*, with a diadem above the crescent[1]. My action caused no surprise to Aurelian who had accepted the compromise temporarily, but was determined to reconquer the East sooner or later. Finally the day came when his wars on the Danube were over and he was ready to deal with Palmyra.

For me it was an hour of crisis. My troops were thinly spread over a large part of the world. I knew that the empire was fragile. I had the support of my people, the Arabs, and yet the Tanūkh, a large federation of Arab tribes, were my enemies. I had the support of the Panhellenists and the native Syrians, but there were many hostile elements from within, such as the Christians of Antioch, who had the power of the Church of Rome behind them, who supported Domnus against my ally and counsellor Bishop Paul of Samosata, and incited against me other Christians in Jerusalem, Alexandria and Caesarea. The 'rationalists' on whom I counted so much were scattered and feeble. The Jews, who fared so well under my rule (and had full religious freedom), to the extent that I even restored their synagogue in Dura-Europos[2] and was rumoured to have become a Jewish convert[3], were my enemies. Their hostility, which was due originally to the destruction of Nehardea, seat of the Babylonian Rabbinical School, in Odainat's first campaign against the Persians, was further sustained by the rivalry of the Jewish merchants with Palmyra.[4] Jewish

1. Cisek, 1994, 103–4.
2. Stoneman, 1992, 152.
3. 'Alī, 1968–73, 109, quotes St Athanasius; Stoneman, 1992, 150.
4. Teixidor, 1997–8, 730.

rancour and spite were such that Rabbi Yohanan b. Nappaḥa of Tiberias had once exclaimed: 'Happy is the man who witnesses the end of Tadmur!' The Jews considered my philosophical ideas heretical, and many fought against me, in the same way that they had fought with the Persians against Odainat. They preferred to be governed by distant Rome than by neighbouring Palmyra, but the real reason behind their hostility was that under the Palmyran empire[5], the Jewish trading colonies on the Euphrates had lost their independence.

Besides hostility, mistrust was also aroused by my so-called pretended conversions to Manicheism[6] and Christianity[7]. In fact, this was the result of my tolerance of groups who were marginalised under Roman rule[8]. In my feverish preparation for war, I learnt of Aurelian's advance from Sirmium to Byzantium, with both his armies, one under the command of his most able general 'Probus' who was in charge of the conquest of Egypt, Provincia Arabia, Palestine and southern Syria[9], the other under his own command and which was to cross Asia Minor and Northern Syria aiming for Palmyra[10]. My intelligence agents informed me that Aurelian had at his disposal twelve legions, auxiliaries and fourteen praetorian cohorts, but he had to

---

5. 'Alī, 1968–73, 109–12; Homo, 1904, 89. On R. Yohanan b. Nappaḥa (who died in AD 279), see Stemberger, 1996, 86.
6. Stoneman, 1992, 150.
7. 'Alī, 1968–73, 112.
8. Watson, 1998, 65.
9. Homo, 1904, 86.
10. Cisek, 1994, 105.

leave some behind, in Italy and on the Danube. In brief, he had the elite of the Danubian troops with thirty years of experience and training, while my young Palmyran army had only the experience of the three campaigns of Odainat, two in Persia and one in Asia Minor, and my campaigns in Provincia Arabia, Egypt and Asia Minor.

I was under stress and very disturbed, and could not shake the feeling of impending doom. I therefore decided, before leaving for Asia Minor and coming face to face with Aurelian, to consult the oracles of Apollo Sarpedon in Cilicia and of Aphacan Venus in Syria on the outcome of the forthcoming war. I had consulted them the previous year and the reply had been positive. I was therefore desolate and in despair when my messengers returned with unfavourable replies[11].

I blindly ignored their warning and did not heed the pronouncement of the gods. But, did I have a choice? I was totally obsessed with defeating the arrogant Aurelian and entering Rome. The news of the fall of Egypt to Probus, who did not find much resistance because I had concentrated my army in Syria, was to be expected, but I still banked on the great showdown with Aurelian when our armies would meet, and I was sure of victory. Meanwhile, Aurelian captured Ancyra without much Palmyran resistance[12] and was in Bithynia which had remained loyal to Rome. The lack of resistance in the cities of Asia Minor was due to the great damage inflicted upon them by the

---

11. Zos., *Hist. Nov.*, 1, 57–8.
12. Zos., *Hist. Nov.*, 1, 50.

incursions of the Goths and the Herules. My strategists decided to pull out our garrisons from Asia Minor so as to meet the Romans on our home territory in Syria,[13] except for the garrison which we left in Tyana to guard the Taurus pass. Tyana offered a very stiff resistance and closed its doors, which so enraged the emperor that he threatened not to leave a single dog alive when he would enter the town. He also pledged to his soldiers that the town would be sacked.

Finally his men found a traitor which enabled them to take the town by surprise. The soldiers reminded Aurelian of his promise, but he refused their request telling them to 'kill all the dogs, for I have promised not to keep a dog alive'[14]. Aurelian did not dare punish the town, afraid of the hostile Panhellenist elements, which he wanted to conciliate and neutralise in his struggle with us[15]. The rumour spread that Aurelian had spared Tyana because he had had a vision of Apollonius of Tyana, asking him to spare the town[16].

We were very disconcerted by the fall of Tyana. Zabadas, my commander-in-chief, did not choose to guard the doors of Syria in the region of Issus, because it was too far from our base of operations and he wanted to draw the Romans to the south in case of a Persian intervention, possibly from Samosata.

---

13. Cisek, 1994, 105.
14. *Hist. Aug., Aurel.*, 22, 2, 5–6; 23, 1–3.
15. *Hist. Aug., Aurel.*, 22, 2, 5–6; 23, 1–3.
16. *Hist. Aug., Aurel.*, 24, 2–6.

Aurelian crossed the Taurus, and captured the Greek towns of Cilicia without a battle. I had the choice of retreating to Palmyra through Apamaea and to fight on our home ground with my army intact, or to face Aurelian now on the Orontes. I chose the second solution, for retreating would have meant sacrificing Antioch, the most important town in my empire after the fall of Alexandria and our base of operations[17].

Aurelian set across the Orontes towards the village of Immae, near Antioch, where I was waiting with Zabadas at the head of my army, which consisted of archers and heavy cavalry, the remnants of two Roman legions, and Arab and Armenian auxiliaries[18].

When Aurelian saw our cavalry, with its heavy arms which gave it confidence and guaranteed it a security much superior to his own, he knew that he could not withstand it with his own light cavalry. He therefore ordered the Roman cavalry not to engage the combat directly but to wait and simulate withdrawal towards the village of Immae. Weighed down by iron, our cavalry followed the supposed retreat of the Romans until our men were tired from the heat and the load which they carried. At that moment, the Romans turned around and charged unexpectedly, thus creating confusion and disorder. There ensued a terrible massacre of our cavalry in which had shone the flower of our aristocracy[19]. The impact of the tragedy was immense, for

---

17. Homo, 1904, 92.
18. Cisek, 1994, 108; Kotula, 1997, 129.
19. Zos., *Hist. Nov.*, 1, 50, 3–9; *Hist. Aug., Aurel.*, 25, 1–3; *Eutrop. Brev.* 9, 13, 19.

Fig. 18 Fragmentary architrave of a portal depicting the eagles of Baʿalšamîn (*in toto* with portal-jamb of Fig. 19 (h 118 cm; l 80 cm; d 24 cm), first century AD, National Archaeological Museum, Damascus (Courtesy of the General Directorate of Antiquities and Museums of the Syrian Arab Republic)

Fig. 19 Right jamb of a portal (to be combined with *Fig. 18*)

Fig. 20 Eagle with outstretched wings and designs of fruit, pine cones and leaves (Photo Julien Charlopin)

Fig. 21 Eagle *en face* flanked by fruit and leaves (Photo Julien Charlopin)

Fig. 22 Hard, white limestone bust of woman (h 60 cm; l 53 cm; d 21 cm), first half of second century AD, Palmyra Museum (Courtesy of the General Directorate of Antiquities and Museums of the Syrian Arab Republic)

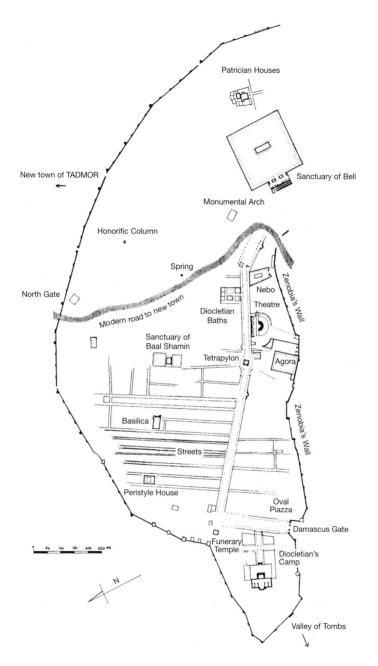

Fig. 23   Plan of Palmyra within 'Zenobia's Wall' (after al-Bounni and Salibi, Courtesy of the General Directorate of Antiquities and Museums of the Syrian Arab Republic)

Fig. 24   After passing through the Valley of Tombs (in the background), the caravan route approaches Palmyra

Fig. 25   The ruins of Palmyra

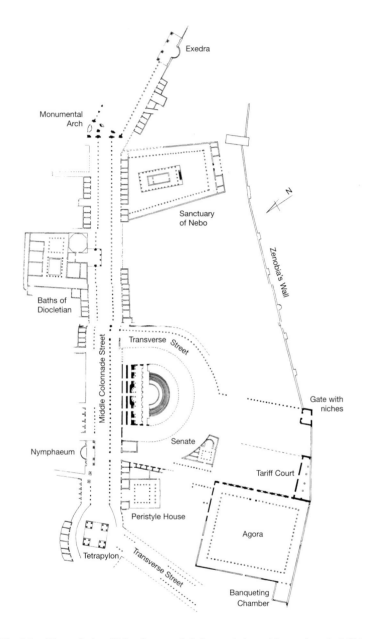

Fig. 26 Plan of the Civic Centre of Palmyra (after al-Bounni and Salibi, Courtesy of the General Directorate of Antiquities and Museums of the Syrian Arab Republic)

Fig. 27   The main segment of the paved Colonnaded Street looking towards the Monumental Arch (Photo Julien Charlopin)

Fig. 28   The Upper Colonnaded Street, looking towards the Tetrapylon (Photo Julien Charlopin)

Fig. 29   Approaching the Tetrapylon from the Upper Colonnaded Street (Photo Julien Charlopin)

who could have foreseen such a reversal of fortune? It was at the moment of this unprecedented disaster that I cried for Odainat – for he would not have allowed such a debacle to befall his army – but I had to keep my bitterness to myself in order not to heap abuse on Zabadas, a shaken man, who overnight grew old.

Zabadas and I retreated with the rest of the army to Antioch before the news of our defeat reached the town, but we were afraid of its fickle citizens. They had already heard of the clemency of Aurelian in Tyana destined to appease the Hellenist components of its population. We were sure that in order to gain Aurelian's favour, our partisans in Palmyra would turn against us and interfere with our withdrawal. We had held Antioch for five years, its inhabitants had enjoyed security, prosperity and a just administration, but, human nature being as it is, we knew that they would drop us with scorn, forget the benefits of our rule and turn to flatter the winner. We also had a hard core of loyal partisans whom we could not leave behind to suffer the vengeance of Aurelian. Zabadas called for a meeting with all our civil and military advisors, to determine our course of action. The meeting went on far into the night and the discussion was tumultuous, disorderly, full of ridicule and laughter until we all agreed on mounting a tragicomic masquerade. The inhabitants of Antioch were frivolous, pleasure-seeking hedonists, and were known for their love of the theatre and spectacles, and so we were going to indulge them. If our farce worked, we would win a safe retreat, but if it floundered, then we would face an uprising against us which would prevent our withdrawal. The tragicomic play was not going to be performed in the amphitheatre, nor in the hippodrome, but in the main streets of Antioch, with all the inhabitants of Antioch as spectators.

The scenario was as follows. In the first act, the shattered remnants of our troops, which had begun entering Antioch, were told to pretend they were victorious. In the second act, our partisans spread the rumour that Aurelian was severely defeated and his army crippled, and a few hours later the even better news that Aurelian was not only defeated but had been taken prisoner, and that we would soon parade the fallen emperor around the streets for all to see.

Excitement was rising, people started to gather on the streets, children left their schools and the country people started arriving from Daphne and villages around Antioch to view the great spectacle. In temples, sacrifices were being offered to the gods in thanksgiving for our victory. Christian followers of our friend the Bishop of Antioch, Paul of Samosata, rang the bells of their churches and sent choirs of young boys and girls into the streets, praising God for our victory. Those of our loyal partisans in Antioch who were in the know, went around the town whipping up enthusiasm for the great drama.

While all the preparations were taking place, we were in a frenzy to find a man who resembled Aurelian. Most people in Antioch had never set eyes on him, but we had to take into consideration veterans who might have fought with him, or served under his command in the Danube area or in Pannonia, and who would recognise him and reveal the enormity of our farce. Zabadas' agents finally found a poor old greying man who had the build of Aurelian and who somehow resembled him. The man was brought to me trembling with fear and I felt a great loathing for him, for he did really look like Aurelian. Zabadas had dressed him in clothes resembling those Aurelian had worn during the battle. I calmed him by giving him a large sum of money. He started to mumble idiotically, so I shut him up and began to coach him for his role: 'All you have to do is to ride a donkey backward and look forlorn and downcast', I said. It was not that difficult for he was miserable by nature.

The situation was so grotesque that I began to laugh, quietly at first, but then I shrieked with laughter. I was true to my erratic nature, for I enjoyed the farce: here I was, having lost Egypt and Asia Minor and just returned from the battlefield after seeing the cavalry, the pride of the Palmyran army, decimated before my eyes, and instead of mourning my soldiers, friends of my youth, whose mutilated bodies hacked by Aurelian and trampled by their own horses were strewn on the grounds of Immae, I sat backstage training an old idiot to mimic Aurelian, a lurid *mise en scène* which could backfire. Stunned by my laughter, the old man, knelt before me, frightened to death, and started gibbering. I controlled my laughter, bade him rise and then called for my attendant to bring a purple cloak. I chose a shabby one from the dozen they brought and threw it around the man's shoulders and propelled him towards my generals and advisors who received him with awe and in silence. Then they broke into whisper: 'It is uncanny, verily he is Aurelian'. The play could now proceed. I looked from the window of the governor's palace at the crowds lining the streets. They were pushing and fighting for places of vantage to see and peer at the humiliated and fallen emperor. They had heard about another Roman emperor, Valerian, captured by the Persians more than twenty years previously near Edessa, but this was the real thing, a live show, a moving open theatre in their own town. Finally they saw the emperor riding backward on an old sick donkey, with his head bowed and they started jeering and mocking him, hurling insults left and right. But the most embarrassing was their cheers for me, Zenobia, Queen and Empress, Victorious, Illustrious, Pious.

On hearing their acclamations, I went away from the window to find a moment of solitude. My tears were falling and I marvelled at the irony of things, and at the fragile veil that divides victory from defeat. What if this comic make-believe were true and I were the victor chasing Aurelian all the way back to Rome. My reverie was interrupted by Zabadas: 'Come and look, my queen. We have succeeded beyond words!', and then he said musingly, 'perhaps falsehoods have more chance of success than truth.' The crowd was turning ugly trying to manhandle the emperor, but our soldiers drew tight around him lest he break down and run away or scream the truth. Torches were lit as the crowds grew thicker. Zabadas turned to me: 'I gave the signal – our soldiers are withdrawing in order but we must leave Antioch while the crowd is busy with the fake Aurelian. Many of our partisans have already fled for fear of reprisals. I am leaving only a rearguard and a detachment in Daphne to cover our retreat.' I nodded that I was ready and looked once more at the town of Antioch which had turned into a huge comic theatre in the space of a day and a night. And I thought to myself: 'Tomorrow this same crowd will be cheering the true Aurelian and their cheers will be exaggerated to cover up for their lapsing today, and they will be hurling insults at the Palmyrans and at Zenobia[20].'

Aurelian entered Antioch after we had retreated through the night, and, as expected, he was received with cheers. He exiled Paul of Samosata and annihilated the detachment of soldiers which we had left behind on the summit of a hill in Daphne, by pushing them into a precipice[21].

Aurelian followed us, marching through Apamaea, Larissa and Arthusa and meeting hardly any resistance until he came to Emesa where he saw our army spread out on the plain, for Zabadas had succeeded in concentrating a powerful army with the bulk of Palmyran troops and the loyal Syrians. Aurelian camped, facing our army with his which consisted of Maeseans Pannonians and a Moorish cavalry[22].

The battle was long and bloody. It started badly for the Romans as their cavalry fled in disorder, but their luck turned and the legions won the day. Again, they fell on our cavalry, and a great massacre followed. Our soldiers were confused and paralysed and began to run, but were downtrodden by the enemy. The plain was full of corpses[23].

---

20. *Zos., Hist. Nov.*, 51, 2; Downey, 1961, 267–8.
21. *Zos., Hist. Nov.*, 1, 52, 1; Will, 1992, 188.
22. *Zos., Hist. Nov.*, 1, 52, 2, 34.
23. *Zos., Hist. Nov.*, 1, 53, 1, 23.

It was cruel – we went from defeat to defeat, first at Immae and now at Emesa. In my despair I summoned a council of war which agreed to evacuate Emesa and renounced further operations in the area, because the Emesans were now hostile. There had always been a rivalry between Emesa and Palmyra, as the sophisticated Emesans considered us to be barbarians. They now sided with the Romans.

We decided to retreat to our fortified city[24] to await help from the Persians. In our haste I left the impedimenta behind, with enough treasure to finance the cost of the war. Aurelian entered Emesa and then followed us to Palmyra.

For Aurelian and his troops, the road was hard and full of obstacles. He had to fight the Arab tribes all the way from Emesa to Palmyra[25], and, besides crossing the desert in the heat and the harassment of Arab tribes, he had to face Syrian and Arab brigands. Moreover, the Beduins prevented provisions from reaching his army.

Palmyra was well fortified. From the height of its walls and funerary towers (Figs. 12 and 13), our archers harassed the Roman troops below. We were well provided with food, but the general staff had not foreseen a long siege. We learnt that the Persians had sent help which had been intercepted on the way[26]. Meanwhile, Aurelian bought a group of Armenian cavalry and some Arab tribes with the gold which I had left behind in Emesa. In spite of everything the morale

---

24. *Zos., Hist. Nov.*, 1, 54, 1.
25. *Hist. Aug., Aurel.*, 26, 1 and 27, 4-5; Février, 1931, 130–1.
26. *Hist. Aug., Aurel.*, 27, 34, 5.

was high, and from the city walls the population of Palmyra mocked and insulted Aurelian. One man mocked him so much that a Persian mercenary beside the emperor aimed an arrow at him which hit him, but the man continued to utter insolent words until he dropped dead before the emperor[27].

As the siege dragged on, we began to lack provisions. Aurelian wrote, asking me to submit, reminding me of our heavy losses near Antioch and Emesa and demanding we yield to the Roman treasury, money, silk, precious stones, horses and camels. For that, he would guarantee my life. I answered that it was for the Romans to submit. Cleopatra had preferred to die rather than to surrender. I did not consider myself defeated and said he should forget his pride[28]. It was for the Romans to submit.

The mood in the besieged town began to change as no assistance was forthcoming. The aristocracy opted for resistance to the end, while the *plebs* and the immigrants started to clamour for surrender. The head of the capitulating party was Septimius Haddûdân the Symposiarch[29].

I began to fear that the will of the Palmyrans would break, and I could not wait any longer for the Persians to cross the desert between the Euphrates and Palmyra and come to our help. I decided to go to them and, like a thief, I stealthily crept through the gates in pitch darkness past the

---

27. *Zos., Hist. Nov.,* 1, 54, 23.
28. *Hist. Aug., Aurel.,* 26, 27, 1; 'Alī, 1968–73, 173; Mommsen, 1985, 807.
29. Will, 1992, 191.

enemy lines, to seek help from the other side of the Euphrates. But there, just at the moment of crossing over, the Roman cavalry caught up with me, and the drama of my life took an unexpected and ugly turn.

CHAPTER V

'Who is Odainat?'

I myself wonder at times: 'Who was Odainat?' In truth, I cannot claim that I ever really knew him, for how can I understand a man who was a thousand men? A man who inhabited worlds beyond my reach, and dimensions beyond my vision, who in his forty-seven years, accomplished deeds that need a hundred lifetimes and was, according to the oracle, 'a fire-breathing lion sent from the sun who will rule the Romans, and the Persians will be weak'[1]. An Arab prince with unfailing generosity, a hardy desert warrior obsessed by his wars and campaigns, a great soldier with legendary courage – a courage worthy of majesty[2].

I do not know where to begin. Perhaps I should start with myself, for in some way I was his creation. It pleased him to play Pygmalion, and, as such, he shaped his fourteen-year-old bride according to his design and his conception of an Arab queen. He schooled me in the arts of war, he taught me riding and soldiering, and, above all, the sport dearest to his heart, hunting, and made me a fit companion for a soldier and a hunter.

---

1. Potter, 1990, 151, quotes the thirteenth Sybilline Oracle.
2. *Hist. Aug., Gall.,* 10, 1, 12, 1.

With what excitement did I always accompany him to the hunt, or to war – for this was my life with him – and the habit continued long after his death (Fig. 14). He was the man that dealt a mortal blow to the mighty Persian Empire in a simple answer to the question which the great king of Persia Sapor had asked in scorn and derision, 'Who is Odainat?' – a question that cost the great king part of his empire, his new conquests in Syria and Mesopotamia, most of his army, his pride and his arrogance, his treasure and (humiliation upon humiliation) his women – wives and concubines!

The only way to understand my husband was to dig into his background, for how could this man, and this man alone, transform a free caravan city at the edge of a desert, from a principality into an Arab kingdom, and finally into the capital of an Oriental Empire and the central city of the East. It was not through magic, and the *ginnaya* (good spirits of a place) of Tadmur did not build it for Odainat. It was both his family and his own iron willpower. 'Our clan, al-Zabbā', he told me, 'owes everything to the Arab emperors, the four Severans and Philip the Arab. For instance, your name Julia Aurelia Septimia: Septimia for Septimius Severus, Julia for the Empress Julia Domna, Aurelia for her son the Emperor Aurelius Caracalla who in 212 gave his *gentilice* and that of his mother as a mark of honour to all Emesans and Palmyrans[3], on the occasion of his constitution which granted Roman citizenship to the

---

3. Rey-Coquais, 1978, 56, n. 166; Sartre-Fauriat, 1997, 974.

people of the empire. Emesa was his mother's native town, and the neighbouring Palmyra he favoured, making it a colony endowed with *Ius Italicum*. Thus, he perpetuated the link which his father Septimius Severus had forged with Palmyra – a remarkable story, for Septimius Severus, the real benefactor of the family[4], came in 193 to Syria to fight Niger. Many towns in Syria, including Palmyra, sided with Niger, but my father with some of his influential friends supported Severus. When Severus won, Hairân, my father, was rewarded by being appointed to the Senate – he was the first Roman senator in the history of the city[5] – and by being given the *gentilice* 'Septimius'. He was also *Ras Tadmur*, Chief of Tadmur. Hairân accompanied Severus on his Parthian Campaign[6], and rendered service to the emperor through his desert scouts. He commanded the Palmyran army, and was chief of the caravans (Fig. 15), but above all he was also chief of the Beduin Arab tribes[7]. The ascendancy of the family was assured. It is of note that a distant ancestor of Odainat, also named Hairân, was a Palmyran priest who resided in Dura-Europos under the Parthians[8].

Odainat succeeded his father Hairân as the head of Palmyra and was made a Roman senator by Philip the Arab during his visit to Syria in 245[9]. After the assassination of Philip the Arab in 249, Odainat took up the challenge in

---

4.   'Alī, 1968–73, 91.
5.   Bowersock, 1983, 129; Gawlikowski, 1985a, 258.
6.   Hitti, 1951, 437.
7.   'Alī, 1968–73, 92.
8.   Starcky and Gawlikowski, 1985, 57.
9.   Starcky and Gawlikowski, 1985, 79.

251, with the support of the Arab tribes and the militia which escorted the caravans[10], of repelling nomad incursions.

He received the title of exarque in 251–2. Already *Clarissimus* and *Consularis* in 257, he was made by Emperor Valerian a governor of Syria-Phoenicia of which Palmyra was part[11]. His other titles were *mrn* (Lord), *Ras Tadmur* and king of Palmyra. In 253, the Persians invaded Syria and were repelled from Emesa by Uranius Antoninus, the Arab pretender to the imperial throne. In 254, Valerian arrived at Antioch which had been abandoned by the Persian troops, and defeated his rival Uranius Antoninus. The Persian invasions of Mesopotamia and Syria continued unabated. In 260, Valerian returned to the East, for Sapor had once more invaded and conquered Carrhae (Harran) and Nisibis, and had besieged Edessa. Valerian agreed to meet with the Persians to negotiate a solution and went with a reduced escort to meet their envoys. Sapor, in flagrant treachery, took him prisoner, with his praetorian prefect and other dignitaries. The population was deported to Persia and Asia Minor was invaded. Northern Syria was conquered and Antioch sacked. Gallienus succeeded Valerian, his imprisoned father.

The capture of Valerian in 260 opened the doors of Syria, and, once again, seven years after the first invasion which was repelled by Uranius Antoninus, Antioch fell and was destroyed. The disaster aroused a lot of emotion in Palmyra,

---

10. Gawlikowski, 1985a, 211; Kotula, 1997, 99.
11. Starcky and Gawlikowski, 1985, 58 and 59.

as it was now surrounded by enemies and its commerce suffered.

The Persians pursued their belligerent action and took Characne on the Persian Gulf, this resulting in the disruption of the caravan routes bringing our commerce to a standstill. Odainat as chief and king of Palmyra, and later governor of Provincia Syria-Phoenicia, was forced to make a move as Roman control over Syria was crumbling. Odainat often spoke of this period as the dormant years. 'I was in a difficult position al-Zabbā", he would say, 'Persian inroads had increased after the murder of Philip the Arab, besides frequent Beduin incursions into Roman territory; and when Uranius Antoninus claimed the empire in Emesa the year Philip was murdered, I did not move against him, to please Rome, for he was a Sampsigeramus, a fellow Arab from the priestly family of Julia Domna, and it was he who had saved Syria from the Persians in 253. Valerian had got rid of him in 254 – by what means I do not know. And then, seven years after his death, the region was falling apart again. I had to draw near Persia, to conciliate Sapor, in order to enable Palmyra to keep in good grace with both powers for the sake of our commerce. The rest of the story you well know!'

I certainly knew the story. I encouraged him to make a move towards Persia, I as well as others from the pro-Persian party who believed that Palmyra's future was with the East, not with the West, for, after all, much of our daily life was modelled on Parthia. Odainat sent an embassy to the retreating Sapor, who had been defeated in Cilicia by the Roman general and praetorian prefect

Ballista[12] who had assembled the remnants of the Roman forces after the capture of Valerian and fought the Persians. I remember the long line of camels, loaded with the most precious gifts our caravans had ever carried, being assembled in great haste, before the Persians crossed the Euphrates, and the Palmyran dignitaries chosen by Odainat for his embassy because of their affinity to Persia being given a letter offering Sapor an alliance. The request was from equal to equal as Palmyra had a great deal to offer, being the only principality in Roman Syria with a militia, trading posts, military forts all along the Euphrates, and immense wealth. On receiving the embassy, Sapor was livid, that a mere Arab sheikh had dared to write to him, he the King of Kings, and offered to conciliate him with gifts! And how dare a nonentity address him thus? 'Who is Odainat?', he shouted himself hoarse, 'If he entertains a hope of mitigating his punishment for daring to address me thus, let him fall prostrate before the foot of our throne, with his hands bound behind his back. Should he hesitate, destitution will be poured on his head, his whole race and country'[13]. Saying this, he threw the precious gifts into the Euphrates.

I cannot ever forget the scene. I never saw Odainat in such a rage, for all his inbuilt tribal code of pride, honour and revenge rose with extreme violence. He was almost speechless. He could only mutter: 'I will make the old goat

---

12. Scarre, 1995, 75 and 179.
13. Malalas, *Chronicon* XII. Kotula (1997, 99), quotes the Byzantine chronicler Peter the Patrician. See also Gibbon, 1934, 260; 'Alī, 1968–73, 93; Mommsen, 1985, 805.

pay for insulting an Arab prince.' The night was long and
dark, and I could neither console nor relieve the tension in
Odainat. I left him alone: he needed silence to regain his
balance. He called me at dawn and spoke with a calm voice
(almost like one of my Sophists making a delicate point).
'Al-Zabbā', he whispered, 'listen carefully and don't
interrupt as you always do.' I let that pass. 'I have thought
out our whole relationship with Persia', he continued. 'First
of all, I have to silence the pro-Persian party in Palmyra, not
by force but by reason, as I have already done with the pro-
Roman party. I myself, as you know, was inclined towards
Parthia. The Parthians favoured our commerce, but the
Sassanids want to dominate it, and use it for their own ends.
Ardashir, their founder, annexed the Arab kingdom of
Characne on the mouth of the Tigris, with Charax Spasinu
its capital, founded by Alexander and rebuilt by an Arab
king, one of our most important trading posts, and our
outlet to the sea. We have had nothing but problems since
the Sassanids took over. Our merchants, especially those
providers of ships and equipment, have now moved their
fleet on the Nile; Alexandria is full of our ship owners[14].
Palmyra has been the centre of jealousy and envy of the
Sassanids ever since the Arabs were at the head of the
Roman government from the Severans to the pretender
Uranius Antoninus, a span of more than sixty years.' Here I
interrupted him by saying: 'Don't you think it is time for the
Arabs to seize the central government again?'. 'No, no,
al-Zabbā, not yet, not now. I have to take on the Persian

---

14. Schwartz, 1976, 143.

Empire – I know your anti-Roman sentiments, but at the moment I need Rome, and Rome needs me even more. I will offer my assistance to Gallienus, and, by Allât, I will deal a blow to the Persian Empire. My father Hairân would have been content to be a client king of Rome, like the Abgarids (the Arab Banū Ghāra) of Edessa but I shall go much, much further – in a few months' time we will be on our way to Ctesiphon.'

Odainat in a sudden reversal of tactics offered his assistance to Gallienus who willingly accepted and passed over the incident of Odainat's embassy to Sapor, for in reality Gallienus had no alternative, with the Persian threat on the one hand, and on the other usurpers and pretenders springing up like mushrooms all over the empire. Odainat had a well-equipped army, with the militia that escorted the caravans across the desert and the remnants of the Roman army that had fled from Edessa, but he was also recruiting feverishly from the desert tents and Syrian villages. All was set for conquering Ctesiphon to punish the arrogant Sapor and to release the aged emperor Valerian from captivity. I sat with Odainat on the war council, I helped in the preparation of the campaign and I accompanied him[15], riding by his side at the head of the army. Our scouts and our cavalry harassed the retreat of a tired, spent, Persian army, attacking them before they were able to cross the Euphrates[16].

---

15. *Hist. Aug.*, *Val.*, 4,3; Février, 1931, 82–3; Starcky and Gawlikowski, 1985, 60.
16. Mommsen, 1985, 804.

Sometimes I had qualms about our adventure, for we were a small desert army facing the forces of a great empire. We could not expect any help from Rome. The remnants of the Roman troops in Syria were tired and disrupted by their defeat, and nobody would logically envisage that we could win against Sapor, he who had defeated the mighty Roman legions in so many battles, but Odainat was sure of himself and of his army. He massed the infantry under the command of his son Herodian, and the cavalry under Zabadas and Zabbaï who were both honoured with the *gentilice* 'Septimius', and we headed in the wake of Sapor towards Ctesiphon. We took the northern route to Samosata, and barred Sapor's passage. Our success was total, Sapor's defeat colossal, and his losses were heavy. We took many prisoners, and Sapor the great king fled before Odainat like a rabbit, with such haste that he left behind his camp intact, with his treasure, his family and concubines[17]. What a night, that of Odainat's first great victory. 'Al-Zabbā', he said calmly, 'the desert is clear of the Persians.' 'Yes', I said, 'except for their dead, their prisoners and their women!.' As a result, the Persians left Dura-Europos which they had captured and destroyed in 256, before the battle of Edessa. It was now Roman again, and a garrison was installed[18].

That night, Odainat spoke to his generals and men resting around the fire under the stars: 'Now my friends, Sapor knows who is Odainat! I took his treasure and shattered his army. I took his concubines. As of this

---

17. Février, 1931, 83; Gagé, 1964, 348; Sartre-Fauriat, 1997, 266.
18. 'Alī, 1968–73, 95.

moment, I am taking the title he was so arrogant about, I am now the King of Kings! I have now taken revenge for his insult to me and to Palmyra, to Valerian and to Rome.' I was amazed at the filial piety[19] he showed towards the old Emperor Valerian, whom he intended to set free at whatever cost, while his son in Rome showed utter indifference – but it would have been too much to expect any moral qualities from the Roman emperor! Odainat followed the fleeing Sapor with artillery, heavy cavalry, archers and siege materials. We crossed the Khabūr river and rode eastwards to Nisibis and Carrhae which were liberated, as well as a great part of Mesopotamia. The joy of the inhabitants was great and the welcome they gave to Odainat and his army was unforgettable. The route to Ctesiphon, Sapor's capital, was now open. Odainat besieged the town and pillaged the surroundings[20]. Nehardea, near Babylon, the seat of Jewish merchants, rivals to Palmyra, was captured[21]. Odainat defeated the Persians under the walls of the city, and as the skirmishes raged daily around the besieged town we received disquieting news from Syria – two usurpers were proclaimed and recognized as emperors in Syria, Egypt and Asia Minor. Palmyra was the only principality which did not recognise them. Gallienus sent word to Odainat asking for help, as he had his hands full in Italy and on the Danube. The situation was serious; we learnt that it had all begun after Valerian's capture in 260. One of his generals, Ballista,

---

19. *Hist. Aug., Gall.*, 10, 2.
20. *Hist. Aug., Gall.*, 12, 1.
21. Sartre-Fauriat, 1997, 266; Sartre, 2001, 176, n. 89.

assembled Roman forces and defeated the Persians in Cilicia, then joined forces with Fulvius Marcianus, governor of the army's warehouses in Samosata, who claimed the imperial throne, but, suffering from a physical disability[22], declared his two sons Marcianus and Quietus co-emperors. When he felt secure and in control of the Orient, he made a bid for the whole empire and accompanied his emperor son Marcianus to fight Gallienus in the West, leaving Quietus in Syria. In the Balkans, the usurpers met Aurelus, Gallienus' general, who defeated them in Illyria. On hearing the news, Odainat lifted the siege of Ctesiphon, and we returned with the army to Syria. I saw how troubled he was, for a hostile emperor on our doorstep would be the end of Palmyra and her dominance over the area. Out of loyalty to Gallienus, he could not allow a usurper in the East. Once he had arrived in Syria, he would not rest, but fought Quietus by detaching from him most Syrian cities, until he cornered and besieged him in his stronghold Emesa. The besieged Emesans who were loyal to Quietus, looked down upon us the Palmyrans as crude and uncultured – 'barefooted Beduins' they called us. So they suffered, since they refused to surrender to the barbarians of Tadmur[23], and their town was destroyed by Odainat.

I was with Odainat during the siege, our camp was on a little promontory which overlooked the town and I could see the crowds of Emesans around the temples, praying, sacrificing to their sun god for victory against the

---

22. Sartre, 2001, 976.
23. 'Alī, 1968–73, 96.

Palmyrans, pleading with the deity to inflict punishment on them. At night, there were processions of priests by torchlight and their prayers were so loud we could hear them at a distance. What irony! For also in our own camp various tribes were praying to their respective gods and many were praying to the sun god, except that in Palmyra we had two of them – Sams, identified with Helios and who shared a sanctuary with Allât; and the sun god Yarhibôl, one of the trinity of Bêl whose priests were outdoing their Emesan colleagues in loud supplication for victory over the Emesans. The situation amused me and I told Odainat flippantly that I found it strange that both Emesans and Palmyrans were praying to the same sun god for victory, which must pose a dilemma for the god who had beautiful and rich temples in both cities. Odainat was not amused and told me sternly: 'I do not know whether to attribute your statement to mischievousness or to pure wickedness. Don't you know that the sun god is a preserve of our tribe – and that he, unlike you, would not have any qualms about which side will win! Anyway, the worship of the sun is a dominant Arab cult and there is no wonder that both towns worship the same god.' In the end, as Odainat had predicted, the sun god gave victory to the Palmyrans[24].

The end came quickly to the pretender Quietus, betrayed and killed by his own praetorian prefect who threw his head from the walls of the city to Odainat. When Odainat left Emesa, the traitor rebelled and declared himself king. Odainat sent his men to the camp and killed him[25].

---

24. 'Alī, 1968–73, 96; Stoneman, 1992, 71 and 74.

The occupation of Emesa left the population very bitter, as they were jealous of the rapid ascendancy of Palmyra. The Orient, however, was freed from the Persians and from usurpers, Gallienus was overjoyed, Mesopotamia was Roman again, and the Orient secured and controlled by the force of one man, Odainat. The Romans who had abandoned the state, had their empire saved in the East by a Palmyran prince, who re-established Roman domination with Palmyran troops and reversed the fortunes of the Roman war. Gallienus entrusted Odainat with the governorship of the East and gave him the title *Imperator Corrector totius Orientis* which implied jurisdiction over the provinces of Asia, Mesopotamia, Syria and Egypt, although Odainat already possessed the East independently[26]. The title most appreciated by Odainat was that of King of Kings which he had torn out of the heart of the king of Persia. Odainat's authority was different from that of ordinary Roman governors and was not dependent on the emperor[27]. Gallienus' decision was well received by the Senate and the Roman people[28] who murmured behind the emperor's back that while he, Gallienus, had abandoned a rocking Roman Empire, it had been saved in the East by Odainat[29]. His jurisdiction covered the entire Orient and Asia Minor with the exception of Bithynia[30]. The Orient having been

---

25. *Hist. Aug., Gall.*, 3, 1, 2; 'Alī, 1968–73, 96.
26. Gibbon, 1934, 241.
27. Mommsen, 1985, 803–04.
28. *Hist. Aug., Gall.*, 13, 1.
29. Eutrop., Brev., 9, 10, 11; *Hist. Aug., Gall.*, 1.1.

recovered, Gallienus held a Triumph and declared himself *Persicus Maximus*[31].

How can I ever recapture those distant days when I basked in the glory of Odainat, when Palmyra became the centre and capital of the Orient, transformed by him from a caravan town to the capital of an Arab principality[32] which now ruled the Roman forces in the East? It is true that some Roman officials resented Odainat's control, but they also enjoyed the security that he had imposed after so much tumult, a security which was not limited to defeating the Persians and checking the Beduins, but included the eradication of bandits and thieves. No one in the East dared dream of challenging Odainat's authority. From the treasure which he had taken from the Persians, he even struck his own coins with his portrait, and that of Gallienus[33].

I was always hovering at his side like his shadow, following his every step, starry-eyed, while he was subtly turning me into a queen. His bearing was so majestic, that I was sure Gallienus would be jealous and afraid of his kingly behaviour[34]. I tried to warn him and was constantly telling him to take heed of Roman treachery, but he had such trust. 'Al-Zabbā', he said, 'I have proved my loyalty. I even sent to Rome the Persian satraps whom I captured in northern

---

30. Commentary by Desbordes and Ratti, 2001, 144 on *Historia Augusta, Gallieni Duo.*
31. Sartre-Fauriat, 1997, 266.
32. Starcky and Gawlikowski 1985, 58.
33. 'Alī, 1968–73, 97.
34. Sartre-Fauriat, 1997, 267.

Syria with the treasures. At any time I could have declared myself emperor of the East, an East which was not given to me gratuitously. I earned it by war and vigilance. Look at the many usurpers and pretenders to the throne – so far I have I counted nineteen, but, by Allât, I am not one of them! Even those who resent me, al-Zabbā', have never had it so good. For the first time the Orient which had been shaken by turbulences since the end of the Severan dynasty is at peace'[35]. 'Odainat', I interrupted, 'I see only jealousy and fear in the hearts of the Romans. They do not trust your motives or believe in your loyalty.' 'Why, why?' he cried.

'You remember, al-Zabbā', that after the assassination of Philip the Arab, the Beduin Arab tribes refrained from incursions into the province of Syria out of respect for me as their desert lord. In a time of extreme tension, my court was open to all, it was a refuge for intellectuals, philosophers, religious men.' 'Odainat', I interrupted, 'your generosity is the talk of men, even in distant lands'. 'Generosity, al-Zabbā', is of the spirit, in tolerance, in acceptance of the other. What men praise is my material generosity – banquets, gifts, donations, perfumes for the baths – but all this is nothing. Generosity is tolerance to the persecuted religious sects, and the end of Christian persecution, freedom for their cult, to build churches and to worship as they please.'

I remember those words of Odainat and lower my head in shame, when I remember people praising me for opening the court to intellectual and religious refugees, for my

---

35. Gawlikowski, 1985a, 251.

tolerance, and they refused to believe me when I replied: 'I only walk on the platform my husband built – for all that you praise me for and attribute to me is the work of Odainat.' No one I remember ever left his court empty-handed, but he was restless; he only felt at ease riding at the head of his army with the Beduins behind him, raising their spears and chanting their war cries. I never had enough time alone with him, and with the years I fell more and more under the spell of his grace, his tall slim stature of a desert warrior and his majestic bearing. He was large in the Arab sense, in that he was above grievances, pettiness and things that poison daily life, as large as the desert that bred him. I wanted him for myself. I was jealous of his sons, Hairân and Herodian[36], especially of Herodian because when Hairân died he gave Herodian the title King of Kings. I was jealous of his companions and resorted to a subterfuge to hold his attention, by discussing our common tribal ancestry for he shared the Arab passion for genealogy (*al-ansāb*) and I shamelessly played on it. Once I set him talking about the subject, he never stopped. 'Remember, al-Zabbā', that we owe our ascendancy to the Severans. Without them we were just one of the many noble clans of Palmyra. I succeeded my father, Hairân[37], who was astute and shrewd enough to side with what looked like a lost cause, that of the Punic-Canaanite African Emperor Septimius Severus. It was in the order of things that when Severus came with his army to fight Niger for the control of the empire, most Syrian towns

---

36. Gawlikowski, 1985a 258.
37. 'Alī, 1968–73, 91–2; Hitti, 1951, 437.

opted for Niger because he was governor of Syria. It was not that Severus was an unknown quantity, for he had been a legate in northern Syria and had a Syrian wife, Julia Domna, a member of the priestly family of Sampsigeramus in Emesa. Few Syrian towns sided with Severus like Laodicaea, Sebaste and Tyre. The majority of the ruling clans in Palmyra opted for Niger, but my father and his friends supported Severus. When Severus won the civil war and became sole master of the Roman Empire, he did not inflict punishment on Palmyra as he had done to Antioch and Neapolis in Palestine for their support of Niger. Hairân, my father who was *Ras Tadmur*, Chief of Tadmur, chief of the Beduin Arab tribes, and at times, chief of the caravan, accompanied Severus on the Parthian campaign, and rendered him invaluable service because of Palmyra's experience in desert warfare, and gave him the aid of the militia which protected the commercial routes. Severus rewarded him by giving him his *gentilice* Septimius and making him a Roman senator, the first in the history of Palmyra[38]. Severus is our benefactor, al-Zabbā', and we must never forget that to him we owe our ascendancy, but do not forget either the other Severans who showed us favour. Caracalla made Palmyra a Roman colony, and Alexander Severus came with his troops on the way to the Parthian war in 233. All the Severan princesses were revered in Palmyra.' I tried to question Odainat on Hairân, a Palmyran priest supposedly one of his ancestors who resided

---

38. Rey-Coquais, 1978, 456, n. 166; Bowersock, 1983; Gawlikowski, 1985a, 258.

in Dura-Europos under the Parthians[39], but Odainat did not have further details about him. We both loved to recall our common tribal ancestor al-'Amālīk and to remember that we both descended from al-Naṣr (in Ḥīra)[40], known as Naswar or Nasores in Palmyra. Odainat was officially Odainat b. Hairân b. Wahaballât b. Nasôr,[41] and I, al-Zabbâ b. 'Umar b. Ḍarb b. Ḥasan b. Odainat b. al-Sumaida b. Ḥāwbar al-'Amālīk[42] (Fig. 16). The name Odainat figured prominently in my ancestry. Our tribal ancestry was a bond between us, for blood ties are very strong amongst Arab tribes. Besides our pedigree, Odainat indulged in talking about his sons. Ḥairân, who was dead, was his favourite. He had been a member of the senatorial order[43] and an exarque, but after Hairân's death Odainat groomed his second son, Herodian, for his succession. Herodian accompanied his father on his two Persian campaigns and in the campaign of Asia Minor, and was assassinated with him. Of our three young sons, Wahaballât, Herannianus (Hairân) and Timolaus (Taîmallât) he saw very little. He was waiting for them to be young men at his side, so that he would turn them into sturdy warriors. Wahaballât, who ruled for five years, was so young when he succeeded his father, that I tried very hard with the artists in the mints of Alexandria and Antioch to make his portrait on the coins look older

39. Starcky and Gawlikowski, 1985, 57.
40. Al-Ṭabarī, *Ta'rikh al-Rusul*, Vol. 2, 31; al-Ma'sūdī, *Murūdj*, Vol. 2, 16; J. 'Alī, 1968–73, 91.
41. The evidence is epigraphic ('Alī, 1968-1973, 91).
42. Al-Ma'sūdī, *Murūdj*, Vol. 2, 19; Ibn Khaldūn, *Ta'rikh*, Vol. 2, 2.
43. Seyrig, 1963, 165.

than the adolescent that he was, but to no avail. I could not force an artist to falsify the portrait of his king. Odainat would have been so proud of him, for he died as his father would have wished, fighting like a king for Palmyra. I am ignorant of the fate of my two younger sons and nobody is able to tell whether they are still alive or dead.

Odainat was reticent about his early life. He only spoke of Philip the Arab who made him senator. He was exarque and senator when I married him in 255 and had spent his time guarding the frontiers during the troubled time which followed the assassinations of Philip the Arab in 249 and Decius in 251. Valerian made him consul and governor of Syria-Phoenicia[44] in 257, between the two Persian invasions and the sack of Antioch in 253 and 260. The old emperor had realized that only Odainat was capable of securing the area, mainly thanks to the Palmyran militia which protected caravans and trading posts all over the East. It was during this period that Odainat transformed our caravan city into a strong, wealthy, Arab principality[45] of which he became king. With the capture of Valerian and the fiasco of his flirt with Sapor, Odainat became a different man. He must have realised that with the potential of Palmyra, arms and money and with numerous Arab tribes of which he was chief, he could go very far in a crumbling Roman Empire, but he was intent on protecting and reviving the empire in the Orient. I and a few of his advisors egged him on to cut his links with the Romans and proclaim an Oriental Arab Empire, but he was adamant.

---

44. Starcky and Gawlikowski, 1985, 249.
45. Gawlikowski, 1985a, 258.

At times he lost his patience and was very angry at my insistence. 'We already have an Arab kingdom, and why do you want to court enmity by proclaiming an Arab Empire? Rome needs me, but I need Rome even more. Or do you ignore the immensity and order of its administration – its governors, officials and legions who obey me as long as I am linked to Rome?'

Odainat was restless. Ruling the Orient with all its problems was not enough for him and life at Court began to annoy him. His wariness of the ever-present Persian threat was chronic, and his alertness through his outposts and his scouts to any sign of movement on their part was an obsession. I often chaffed him about this constant restlessness. 'You are only at home, Odainat, in one of your thousand roles', I said. 'And which one is that?,' he asked. 'Your role as an Arab chief, riding your horse in the battlefield, brandishing your sword, with the Arabs behind you'. 'By Allât, Arsu and 'Azîzu, you are right, al-Zabbā', but you too have the same malady. You are aching for the battlefield.' 'Am I not of your blood? Have I not been schooled by you?' I asked. 'I am contrite, al-Zabbā', I have an unfinished task. I had to lift the siege of Ctesiphon when the town was about to fall and return to fight the cursed usurper. I have to go back – with a larger force. I still have a score to settle with Sapor. It is four years since I left Ctesiphon, and the occupation of Characne where the Tigris and the Euphrates meet has affected our commerce. How these Sassanids envy the prosperity of Palmyra, but their jealousy is not new; it goes back to the time

---

46. Février, 1931, 73.

when the Arabs were at the head of the Roman Empire[46]. Our merchants and traders who have long been settled in Babylon, Spasinu Charax and Vologesias, suffer tremendously under Sassanid control. How could I leave them to their fate? Gone are the days when a Palmyran served as a satrap under Meerdates, king of Spasinu Charax[47], but fortunately we still have our secret and open contacts with our countrymen in trading posts along the major routes. Palmyran merchants never lose their identity, in the same way that our archers who serve in the Roman army all over the world keep their identity distinct and maintain their links with their native city.[48] We are now integrating them into the Palmyran army.' 'Odainat,' I interrupted, 'you are then preparing for war? You want to free Valerian from the Persians. I know that his captivity has been gnawing at you. Your filial piety is wonderful, while his own son Gallienus shows no such zeal and has left him to rot!'. 'Al-Zabbā,' he cried angrily, 'the emperor has all the Barbarians in the West to contend with, and a new usurper every day. The East is my domain and I assume that responsibility.' I was silenced. I was chastised. A few days later we learnt that the seventy-year-old emperor had been humiliated and tortured by Sapor on horseback riding over Valerian's hands[49]. I thought to myself that this second campaign would be easier. Odainat had a Roman

---

47. Millar, 1996, 332.
48. Millar, 1996, 334.
49. *Hist. Aug., Gall.,* 5, 1.
50. Février, 1931, 87.

contingent with artillery and siege material[50], besides the heavy Palmyran cavalry, the archers, and the Arab tribes. I was with him on this second campaign as well as his son Herodian. We crossed the Khabūr river, and the route to Ctesiphon was open. The siege was long. Odainat repeatedly defeated the Persians at the walls of the city[51].

Sapor wanted peace but Odainat wanted to free Valerian[52] and was frustrated; he could not attack Characne which was too far from his operational base[53].

One night he came to my tent with a face so sombre I thought he was ill. I waited till he sat down and began to speak calmly: 'Al-Zabbā', have I lacked in reverence or in sacrifice to our ancestral gods that they decree twice I should lift the siege of Ctesiphon'? I was aghast: 'What ill news have you received Odainat? Has Egypt revolted or is it Antioch?' 'It is worse than that al-Zabbā', it is the barbarian Goths. They have crossed the Black Sea and reached Pontus. They attacked Bithynia and are now ravaging Asia Minor.' I understood his dilemma. He was responsible for the security of Asia Minor and could not allow the Goths to terrorise the population and destroy his domain. Odainat did not hesitate one moment; his duty was first for the welfare of the people he governed, and punishing Sapor would come later. He lifted the siege for the second time, regrouped the army, and started back. On arrival in Syria he sent me with an escort to Palmyra, and

---

51. *Hist. Aug., Gall.,* 10, 6 and 7.
52. 'Alī, 1968–73, 98.
53. Février, 1931, 88.

refused to let his army rest, but continued the march to Cappadocia. The expedition was successful against the Gothic plunderers, who retreated on his arrival. He observed all the forms towards Rome and proved his loyalty by sending the enemy officers who had been taken prisoner, and the treasures to the emperor[54]. He then decided to return immediately to Ctesiphon.

Odainat's success and fame were so established that those in Rome trembled. Gallienus was deeply jealous because he acted like a king. In fact, he acted like a Roman emperor, distributing titles and bounty. The Romans could not tolerate that Palmyra had become the first city of the Orient, overshadowing Antioch, Apamea, Emesa, Bostra and Alexandria. I was sure that political intrigue was fermenting in Rome against Odainat, but he would not heed my suspicions, for he was honourable and loyal and expected the same from others, nor would he listen to anything said against his son Herodian's frivolity. The latter's behaviour was shocking as he swaggered about, especially after Odainat had given him the title King of Kings. Odainat's indulgence towards his son was intolerable for Herodian was the most effeminate of men, and adorned his tents and pavilions with embroidered cloth and brocade silk in imitation of the Persians. Odainat loaded him with money, jewels and concubines, and when I remonstrated with him, he told me not to be a wicked stepmother and increased his solicitude[55].

---

54. *Hist. Aug., Gall.,* 10, 6, 7.
55. *Hist. Aug., Tyr. Trig.,* 16, 1–3.

Odainat returned from Asia Minor after he had repelled the Goths and wished to let his army rest for a few days before rejoining the route to Ctesiphon. I was to meet him in Emesa. How could I have guessed that I would only see him dead?

The conspiracy was arranged by Cocceius Rufinus, governor of Arabia[56], on the orders of the emperor. Rufinus played on the rancour of a vindictive, spiteful cousin, Maeonius, who succumbed to the temptation which the Romans offered him for eliminating Odainat and his son and heir, so that he could have access to the throne. Neither he nor his Roman masters bothered to take account of me, his wife, or of his other sons as successors, for according to their estimation I was only a feeble woman with minor sons.

The deed took place at a fatal banquet in Emesa after a day's hunt. During the meal, the treacherous murderer and his friends attacked and killed both Odainat and Herodian. It suited the Romans to clothe the heinous deed as a domestic incident in which Odainat had insulted his cousin during the hunt, but they did not stop at that. They even spread rumours that I, Zenobia, had intrigued to kill him in order to ensure the succession for my son Wahaballât.

They killed him at the height of his power, because they suspected his loyalty, although he did not claim nor seize the empire as nineteen pretenders had attempted in the reign of Gallienus. He alone had the mint of Antioch strike coins in the name of the emperor[57], he alone had a sense of honour

---

56. *Hist. Aug., Gall.,* 3, 2; Gawlikowski (1985a, 259–261) cites the anonymous continuation of Dio's *Roman History.*
57. Will, 1992, 185.

and the power to protect the majesty of Rome. Gallienus could not face the 'lion from the sun' in battle, so he resorted to a shameful conspiracy. Who can ever fill the empty space he left? Who can arrive at his supremacy? But I could not give way to grief. I said to myself: 'Lament no more, Zenobia', for the whole region was in jeopardy and the whole military and diplomatic edifice which Odainat had built was in danger of collapse.

I was in a frenzy. I vowed that I would avenge his death, make the Romans pay dearly for their cowardly treachery. I grieved, I had not been with him on that fatal day in Emesa (he always said that my presence brought him luck), and on that day his luck failed and his stars were dimmed.

I vowed to the 'god who hears, whose name is blessed forever, the merciful,' that I would not let Odainat's life-work crumble. I remembered his words: 'Never forget al-Zabbā' that Tadmur is not only a city, but that its soul is in the Arab tents. Our strength lies in the support of the Arab tribes of the deserts of Syria and Mesopotamia.'

The words have a different resonance now, for our enemies the Tanūkh have started to raise their heads after the assassination, to take advantage of the confusion and of a feeble woman, to bid for Arab leadership, a thing they could never have envisaged in Odainat's lifetime.

On hearing the news, I summoned a war council, for Maeonius had declared himself king before the army. I therefore sent word to Emesa to put him to death,[58] and before anybody could bat an eyelid, I had Wahaballât

---

58. *Hist. Aug., Gall.,* 33, 10, 1.

declared king with all his father's titles while I assumed the regency as queen.

The change took place at such speed that it left everybody breathless. Having got rid of Maeonius, I heard rumblings from the Palmyran nobles who wanted to regain the ascendancy over Palmyra which they had lost to our family since the time of Severus, forgetting that Odainat had made a desert city into the seat of a vast empire. At times I stopped to think of the slight young girl who had been chosen by the Chief of Tadmur as a bride. And I remembered the metamorphosis he wrought upon that girl, beginning her education by riding, hunting, and the art of war, both Persian and Roman, each with different tactics and style, and the desert warfare with its speed in movement and its element of surprise (Fig. 17). 'I will teach you the art of war, al-Zabbắ. I leave it to the Sophists who flock to our Court to teach you philosophy.' As to Arabic, he accompanied me to the Arab tents where poetry was recited and proverbs and tales told and retold from one generation to another. It was there that I learnt the science of genealogy and the interrelationships between the various tribes. He made me meet all his allies, Egyptians, Armenians and Blemmyes.

He taught me to take risks, to seek calculated adventure. 'Remember', he said, 'that without risks Palmyra would have remained a nondescript, rich caravan city, instead of becoming the capital of an empire. Remember that I took on the mighty Persian Empire against everybody's advice and now you are itching and egging me on to challenge Rome. One empire at a time, al-Zabbắ, not both of them.' Little did my beloved Odainat dream that I would take on Rome and gamble with the very existence of Palmyra.

Explanatory Note:

The Severans and Syrian Cities

Septimius Severus, a Phoenician-Canaanite, a Western Semite who had become the master of Rome, allied himself with and favoured Semitic Arab princes in the East, particularly those of Palmyra. The Severans that followed him demonstrated that the leadership of the Roman Empire was rooted in Africa and Asia. They elevated the Oriental provinces to the zenith of prosperity and magnificence, building new monuments, embellishing old ones, and repairing roads from Palmyra to Emesa, Baalbek to Aleppo, Laodicea to Tyre, as well as the great Phoenician coast-road. In turn, they were honoured by dedications, statues and coinage.

Under the Severans, Palmyra became a colony with Italian rights. In the temple of Bêl a citizen placed a dedication to the emperor and his two sons. In the *agora* was another dedication to the emperor, his wife and sons, as well as busts of Severus and Julia Domna. Palmyra reached the height of its power under Severan rule, but started to militarise after it had lost imperial protection[1].

Palmyra was not the only beneficiary. Other Syrian cities also benefited largely from Severan protection. Tyre became a colony with Italian rights, and Baalbek (Heliopolis) a colony with Italian privileges. Its sanctuary was enlarged and a statue of the emperor was set up in the shrine which

---

1. Perowne, 1962, 79–80; Gagé, 1964, 148.

was the abode of the sun god. The building of the great temples was at last completed and the *propylaea* were dedicated to Caracalla and Julia Domna Augusta. Caracalla founded games at Baalbek. Sebaste in Palestine became a colony and was endowed with a temple, a theatre, a stadium and a colonnaded street. The upper aqueduct of Aelia (Jerusalem) was repaired. Lydda (Diospolis) whose population numbered Christians and Jews, reverted to paganism and was rededicated to Zeus. Beit Jibrin (Eleutheropolis) became a colony and a metropolis of southern Palestine. Tyre, Acre (Ptolemaïs) and Damascus were embellished. Loadicaea became a colony and a metropolis and was endowed with an avenue in the shape of a grand colonnaded portico. The Severans were honoured by the Syrian towns in different ways. Julia Domna was honoured with coinage in Tyre, Tripolis, Byblos, Ptolemaïs, Bostra, Rabbath-Moab, Petra, Diospolis, Aelia, Gaza and Neapolis. Inscriptions in honour of the dynasty were found in Jarash (Gerasa) and Bostra. Dedications by soldiers, veterans, shepherds and peasants for the health and success of Caracalla, who was very popular in Syria, were numerous. Shrines were set for up for Caracalla in Atil and Zabīrah in the Hawrân. At Der'a, a column and a statue of victory were erected in his honour[2].

---

2. Perowne, 1962, 106–7 and 109.

CHAPTER VI

Come, Eagle of Jupiter

Come bird, make haste, eagle of Jupiter, fly me to the heavens, fly me to the sun[1]. Speak to me, bird of heaven, for you awaken memories of another bird, so long, long ago (Figs. 18 and 19). You must remember, eagle of Jupiter, for they say you are ageless and timeless, the magic words of my childhood 'Speak bird, speak,' the prelude to the enchantment of a tale, a myth, an adventure, the opening formula without which no respectable age-old Arab tale could begin. Ah, words of music, words of joy, how could I describe the thrill they gave, but like everything else in life a price had to be paid. I had to spend the next day pleading with the old hag, the one-eyed retainer, for another evening tale, and when the time came she would keep me waiting on tenderhooks, until she would deign to begin, muttering unintelligible words, probably maledictions, while easing her heavy bloated body onto the couch. I swear I could hear the cracking of her bones, but then the process

---

1. Ingholt discovered a tomb with a ceiling decorated with a brown, painted eagle. According to ancient beliefs, it is this bird which carried the soul of the deceased to the sun (al-Bounni and al-As'ad, 1987, 43 and 45).

of clearing her throat, wiping her only eye and rubbing her nose would begin and all I could do was to move nearer and to say aloud: 'Say it, bird'! She always feigned anger at my infringing on her prerogative and chided me by saying: 'Cannot you wait a minute child?', before to my great joy she would utter 'Speak, bird, speak'. It was in the blue hour of the night that the tale ended, but I cannot recall when it began. On the morrow, I spent part of the day trying to find a replacement for the old hag, by begging my aunts, my nurses, my slaves for the evening tale. Meanwhile, my mother was lobbied by my nurses to make me stop the habit of refusing to go to bed without a tale, but she gently refused, reproaching them: 'Let the child be, if your tales are exhausted, invent new ones and fabricate dreams, you know my heart tells me that the child herself will one day be the subject of tales.'

Alas, bird of heaven, my childhood and its tales are gone and here I wait for you to fly my *naphša* on your wings. Tell me bird, why this delay? Is it because I have not said it all? 'He who hears, blessed be his name forever' allowed me to speak, but there are mysteries of the heart that cannot be revealed, words that cannot be spoken. Palmyra was destroyed but who would believe that I was only a tool, an instrument for its destruction? Palmyra was destroyed, but the struggle for freedom is beyond destruction. It will rise again and again with every generation until liberty from Rome is achieved. My only role was to hasten the process, for the Romans would have destroyed Palmyra with or without me. They could not accept a strong, prosperous and militarised Arab state. They only tolerated it when it served their imperial purpose, for it policed Roman frontiers and checked their enemies. They annexed Nabatea a century and a half before us, although Nabatea never threatened them as Palmyra did. Neither did Iturea nor Edessa. But they destroyed them just the same. I actually struck them at the moment in time, when they were on the verge of striking me and I succeeded beyond measure, but now it is all dust and ashes.

Yes, bird, I have already spoken of Zenobia, the wife and companion of Odainat, the mother and regent of Wahaballât, the general who outwitted and outflanked the enemy, the queen who walked on a tightrope between two empires, but I have not spoken of the other Zenobia, the Platonist, the lover of philosophy, and perhaps this Zenobia is the most real of all. I have often said that Odainat, the warrior-sheikh who clung to a strict code of honour, was a thousand men in one, but I, Zenobia Septimia, am a performer who played a thousand roles, and each role I enacted seemed real for the moment in time in which it was played.

I will tell you my secret, bird of Jupiter, bird of Zeus. I will give you the answer to the questions that people of my empire often asked. 'How could the queen withstand defeat and ruin?. How could she bear the catastrophe of Immae, and the flower of Palmyran youth lying mutilated in foreign fields? How could she bear the massacre of Emesa, the retreat, the siege, the loss of empire, kingdom, treasures and riches?' Legitimate questions for which there no answer. The few who were allowed to see in captivity left my cell whispering aloud, with their tears falling: 'How could she take this humiliation? She has nothing, but absolutely nothing left.'

Yes, bird, I lost all, nothing is left. The edifice I built after a long, thorny struggle is gone with the wind, and my life – ah, that was hard! One obstacle after another. It was not easy to marry a mighty Arabian chief with two grown-up sons who resented me. Nor was it easy to rise up to his level in peace or in war, and later, when he was gone, I was a free target for his enemies who saw in me nothing but a feeble woman with pretensions. But I showed them what a feeble woman can do and deprived them of the pleasure of attacking my virtue and my honour, for a woman's virtue is the first target for jealous men. How they searched in vain to find me a lover! How they schemed and plotted to smear my character! But I always won. My kin, the Arab tribes, far in the desert, sang my virtue, and soldiers, whether allies or enemies, testified to my courage. I not only fought with my troops, I walked with them, I ate and drank with them. It is hard, bird, to bear the downfall (Figs. 20 and 21).

The answer, bird of heaven, is that all my life I was play-acting. I was only a character on a stage and I played my roles to perfection. I was but a toy, playing with other toys. It is confusing, bird, so let me explain.

I was a lover of philosophy, verily, it was my one true role. What were my other roles you ask? The whole world knows those, bird – politics, empire and war in which I was the leading actress, and Aurelian the Roman emperor, was the villain of the play.

You know, bird, that I was a student of Cassius Longinus who infused me with Platonic ideas and Platonic mirages and made of me a Neoplatonist[2]. My court became the centre for the Neoplatonists who were mainly Oriental Sophists. Longinus opened for me the doors of thought and vision of other Neoplatonists, mainly of his rival Plotinus with whom he disagreed on some points of doctrine. Plotinus was an Egyptian from Lycopolis (Asiūt), five years older than Longinus[3] who hailed from Emesa. Both were Orientals. Contrary to Longinus, who grew up in an intellectual milieu and had a Sophist uncle, Plotinus came late to philosophy when he was twenty-eight years old. He studied in Alexandria with many masters who left him unsatisfied and dejected, until he was led to Ammonius Saccas, with whom he stayed until he joined the emperor Gordian and his Praetorian Prefect Philip the Arab in their campaign against the Persians in Mesopotamia, for the purpose of studying Indian and Persian philosophy.

After the campaign, when Plotinus was forty years old, he went to Rome, in the reign of Philip the Arab. There, he was respected and venerated by senators, by men and women from the Roman aristocracy. He was given the use of a house by a wealthy widow Gemina, and in summer a villa in Campania by an Arab doctor, Zethos, to whom he was deeply attached and whom he might have known from his Alexandrian days. He was later introduced to the

---

2. Plotinus would have been surprised at being thought the founder of a new school, Neoplatonism. He considered himself simply a Platonist, without prefix or qualifications – an interpreter of Plato who in his view possessed the truth, the whole truth. See Henry, 1991, lxvii.

3. Plotinus was born in AD 205; Longinus in 210.

Emperor Gallienus and his wife Solinina who honoured and venerated him.

Plotinus proposed to the emperor to establish a city in Campania to be ruled according to the laws of Plato, but the scheme was aborted because of jealousy and spite at court[4]. I often teased Longinus about this, telling him while Plotinus failed to form a city of philosophers in Italy, he already had one in Palmyra!

Plotinus, a mystic who was also a rationalist for whom the intelligible world was more real than the physical[5], seemed ashamed of being in the physical body[6]. He was endowed with a remarkable gift of penetrating the human character and could also foretell the future. He had a thorough knowledge of geometry, mechanics, optics and music[7].

Longinus introduced me to the works and ideas of the philosophers of our time who have left their theories in writing, the Platonists Euecledes, Democritus and Proclinius, the Stoics Themistocles and Phoibion, the Peripatetic Heliodorus of Alexandria, the Platonists who did not write their teachings and doctrines, Ammonius and Origen, and many Stoic teachers who refrained from writing. But of all these Sophists, according to Longinus, only Plotinus and G. Amelius his disciple and associate introduced a method of their own and are worthy of study. Plotinus set the principles of Pythagoras and of Plato in a clearer light than

4. Dillon, 1991, lxxxvii; Porphyry of Gaza, *Vita Plotini* 7, transl. MacKenna, 1991, cviii.
5. Porph. Gaz., *Vit. Plot.*, 11–12 transl. MacKenna, 1991, cxi–cxii.
6. Porph. Gaz., *Vit. Plot.*, 1 transl. MacKenna, 1991, ciii.
7. Porph. Gaz., *Vit. Plot.*, 11 transl. MacKenna, 1991, cxi.

anyone before him. Longinus also refuted the idea spread by some jealous Greek philosophers that Plotinus appropriated his ideas from the philosopher Numenius of Apamea[8].

Longinus, the former head of the Platonic Academy of Athens who was being eclipsed by Plotinus in Rome and who differed from him on points of doctrine and was not convinced by his theories, was generous to his rival, for he ranked him above all others and considered him worthy of the deepest veneration, while Plotinus said of him: 'Longinus is a man of letters, but in no sense a philosopher[9]'. Longinus, however, was large enough to ask his former disciple Porphyry (who left him because he preferred the system of his rival) to send him a complete set of the works of Plotinus to Palmyra or to bring them himself, for he was eager to examine the various treatises and was full of admiration for a man with whom he did not agree[10].

I say all this, bird, to show how sublime Longinus was. It was thus that I was introduced to the works of Plotinus, which I often discussed with Amelius, his heir apparent for eighteen years, until he was displaced by Porphyry. It was then that he came to Apamea to establish his Neoplatonic school.

I read each treatise with an inner recognition, for they left a deep echo in my heart and in my mind. The delight, and consolation they gave to a confused and worried queen was beyond measure, for Plotinus possessed by birth

---

8. Porph. Gaz., *Vit. Plot.*, 17 and 20 transl. MacKenna, 1991, cxiv and cxviii–cxix.
9. Porph. Gaz., *Vit. Plot.*, 14 transl. MacKenna, 1991, cxiii.
10. Porph. Gaz., *Vit. Plot.*, 19 transl. MacKenna, 1991, cxvii.

something more than is accorded to other men[11]. I began to see the world with the Platonist eyes of Longinus and Plotinus, but I must admit that I could not always follow or understand Plotinus so I selected what suited me. Longinus, my mentor, took exception to my method and wanted me to study the whole work in depth, but I had to remind him gently, if perchance he had forgotten, that I had another job to do! And yet within myself I wished I could devote more time to philosophy, but being what I am I could only select what gave me delight. From Plotinus I learnt by heart and repeated like a litany his thoughts on Beauty, for he follows Plato in locating the essence of beauty in a non-material principle[12], for beauty is less in the symmetry of the face than in the flash of light that shines in that symmetry, for it is the light that is beautiful. Again, since the one face constant in symmetry appears sometimes fair and sometimes not, can we doubt that Beauty is something more than symmetry, that symmetry itself owes its beauty to a remoter principle?[13]. The soul includes a faculty peculiarly addressed to Beauty, or the soul itself affirms the beautiful where it finds something which accords with the Ideal-Form within itself[14]. How often have I repeated his words to enable me to regain my composure when men made me bitter and angry: 'Man is a beautiful poem and a noble creation, as perfect as the scheme allows.'[15]

---

11. Porph. Gaz., *Vit. Plot.*, 10 transl. MacKenna, 1991, lx.
12. Henry, 1991, xlix.
13. Plotinus, *Enneads* I, 6 (Beauty), 1 transl. MacKenna, 1991, 46.
14. Plot., *Enn.*, I, 6 (Beauty), 3 transl. MacKenna, 1991, 48.
15. Plot., *Enn.*, III, 2 (Providence), 1, 9 and 15 in Loriot and Nony, 1997, 260.

Patience, heavenly bird, for here is my secret at last. I could bear war, calamities and misfortune because Plotinus taught me that the world is a stage, that all was play-acting, that war, murders, death, the reduction and sacking of cities all must be to us just a spectacle in the changing scenes of a play, all is but the varied incident of a plot, costume on and off, acted grief and lament. For on earth in all succession of life, it is not the soul but the shadow of man that grieves and complains and acts out the plot on this world stage. All this is the doing of man, never perceiving that in his weeping and his graver doings alike, he is but at play[16]. All human intentions are but play. Death is nothing so terrible. To die in wars and battles is to forestall a little the coming of old age; it is to part earlier in order to come back sooner. As to the misfortunes that accompany life, the loss of property for instance, the loser will see that there was a time when the property was not his, that the robbers will in turn lose it to others, for to retain property is a greater loss than to forfeit it[17].

I may be accused, heavenly bird, of interpreting Plotinus' ideas to justify my deeds, especially my wars, but the vision he gave of life was my life, bird, as if he had foreseen my deeds and misfortunes. I never met Plotinus, he died while I was at the height of my power and when the whole world was my stage, but his teaching gave me a foretaste of the stages and states of union with the absolute. He

---

16. Plot., *Enn.*, III, 2 (Providence), 15 transl. MacKenna, 1991, 151.
17. Plot., *Enn.*, III, 2 (Providence), 15 transl. MacKenna, 1991, 150–1.

rediscovered and revitalised the doctrine of the immortality of the soul which goes back to Plato and Socrates[18]. As for me, the immortality of the soul was part of the religion of Tadmur, the tomb was only the abode of the carnal body, while the soul escaped to the sun. This was portrayed in the frescoes painted in tombs of the legend of Achilles and the eagle carrying Ganymede[19], as you will carry me, bird of Jupiter. How this brings back the intense religious life of Tadmur, with processions carrying the image of the deity from the temples through the colonnaded street – the tumult, the excitement, the exultation of the throng, the loud invocations that reached the heavens. Yes, bird, I remember the fresco on the ceiling of the temple of Bêl, with the procession of the tabernacle, a dome in red leather on a camel, and the veiled women who accompanied it and who could not join the ceremony without covering their hair[20]. Verily when I look back at my life on earth I am grateful for the Platonists, for Longinus and Plotinus, who helped me carry my violent personal suffering as well as I could, for in all my pain I asked no pity because there was always the radiance of the inner soul, untroubled, like the light in a lantern when fierce gusts beat about it in a wild turmoil of wind and tempest[21].

---

18. Henry, 1991, lxix.
19. The Tomb of the Three Brothers Starcky, 1960, 1091; Browning, 1979, 206 and 209–10.
20. Dussaud, 1955, 116–7.
21. Plot., *Enn.*, I, 4 (Happiness), 1 transl. MacKenna, 1991, 30.

All this, my past life, is fading fast, bird of Jupiter, heavenly bird. And as you see, the soul of Zenobia, an aspiring Platonist, once upon a time queen of Tadmur, is ready to fly.

Fig. 30   The Tetrapylon (Photo Julien Charlopin)

Fig. 31   The theatre viewed from the south (Photo Julien Charlopin)

Fig. 32   The *scaena frons* of the theatre viewed from the south (Photo Julien Charlopin)

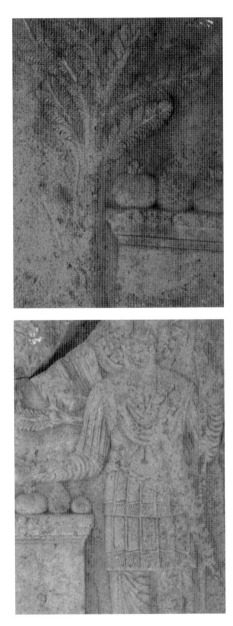

Figs. 33 and 34 The God Yarhibôl as a Palmyran warrior in Parthian dress next to an altar heaped with offerings of pomegranates and pine cones (Photo Julien Charlopin)

Fig. 35   The peristyle-court in the house of a wealthy Palmyran (Photo Reine Jauffret)

Fig. 36   The entrance portal to the Temple of Bêl incorporated into the peristyle surrounding the structure (Photo Julien Charlopin)

Fig. 37   The 'Zodiac ceiling' of the northern *adyton* of the Temple of Bêl (Photo Julien Charlopin)

Fig. 38   The ceiling of the southern *adyton* of the Temple of Bêl, carved with a large acanthus and lotus leaves' fleuron design surrounded by a broad meander-band (Photo Julien Charlopin)

Fig. 39 Limestone low-relief carving (h 23 cm; l 18 cm) depicting a camel at rest, second to third century AD, Palmyra Museum (Courtesy of the General Directorate of Antiquities and Museums of the Syrian Arab Republic)

Fig. 40 Hard limestone relief (h 90 cm; l 68 cm; d 12 cm) from one of the beams of the temple of Bêl depicting veiled women accompanying a procession, first half of the first century AD, National Archaeological Museum, Damascus (Courtesy of the General Directorate of Antiquities and Museums of the Syrian Arab Republic)

Fig. 41 Limestone architrave from the Temple of Ba'alšamîn, first century AD, Palmyra Museum (Photo Studio Zouhabi, Palmyra)

Fig. 42 The Temple of Ba'alsamîn in Palmyra, first century AD (Photo Studio Zouhabi, Palmyra)

Fig. 43 Priests at a funerary banquet in hard, white limestone (h 114 cm; l 164 cm), ca AD 210–40, Palmyra Museum (Courtesy of the General Directorate of Antiquities and Museums of the Syrian Arab Republic)

Fig. 44 Hard, white limestone funerary stele (h 81 cm; w 38 cm) depicting the bearer of a sacrificial ram, second to third century AD, Palmyra Museum (Courtesy of the General Directorate of Antiquities and Museums of the Syrian Arab Republic)

Fig. 45 Hard, white limestone funerary stele (h 96 cm; w 41 cm) depicting the bearer of a ram as a sacrificial offering, second century AD, Palmyra Museum (Courtesy of the General Directorate of Antiquities and Museums of the Syrian Arab Republic)

CHAPTER VII

Legends and Arabic Traditions

Very few figures can rival Zenobia, shrouded in fantasy and legend, as one of the most romantic figures in history. Her tragic persona invaded both Eastern and Western literature, she inspired politicians, artists, painters, craftsmen and poets, and became the subject of historical fiction, plays and poems and even tapestries. Her fame has been gaining momentum for more than one thousand seven hundred years.

Western literature is full of Zenobia. Boccacio included her in his book of great personalities and Petrarch honoured her likewise. In Britain she became the idol of the Victorian age, mainly thanks to Lady Hester Stanhope's theatrical visit to Palmyra in 1813 in search of the remnants of Zenobia's greatness[1]. In the seventeenth and eighteenth centuries operas were consecrated to her and the Tsarina Catherine I tried to rival the splendour of her court. It is beyond the scope of this study to enumerate the Western poets, artists, playwrights, military men and novelists who were inspired by her life and achievements – they are legion.

---

1. Stoneman, 1992, 1; Kotula, 1997, 125.

Historians and archaeologists were not immune to her legend nor to the sad end of her city. On visiting Palmyra in the eighteenth century, Volney mused: 'Here, I said to myself, an opulent city once flourished, and now a mournful skeleton is all that subsists – thus perish the works of men and thus do nations and empires vanish.[2]'

Serious archaeological research began at the end of the nineteenth century, with the Russian Prince Abamalek Lazareff shipping the Palmyra tariff stone to St Petersburg in 1884. A German archaeological mission excavated in 1902–17, the French Cantineau and Starcky followed after the first world war, to be replaced later by Danes, Americans and more recently by Michaelowski and Gawlikowski directing the Polish mission. Concurrently, excavations have also been conducted by the General Directorate of Antiquities and Museums of the Arab Republic of Syria.

In the East, Zenobia still holds the imagination. The legend of her downfall, which is similar to that of the Trojan horse is so widely spread that almost every Arab schoolchild from the Atlantic to the Gulf can recite the line of poetry she allegedly uttered on that fateful day when the caravan loaded with soldiers in the guise of merchandise entered the city: 'Why are the camels proceeding so slow? Is it iron they carry, or men, to and fro?'

The Arabic tradition of Zenobia is irreconcilable with the Western Classical tradition. The discrepancy between the historical Zenobia, queen of Tadmur, and al-Zabbā', queen of Arab tribes in northern Syria, led one scholar,

---

2.   Stoneman, 1992, 13.

A. al-Bounni, to presume that they were two different personalities. His theory rests on their difference of objectives, Zenobia fighting the Romans and al-Zabbā' fighting the Tanūkh; Zenobia being married and al-Zabbā' not; al-Zabbā's father being a king and Zenobia's father not. Al-Bounni, however, admits that they lived in the same period[3]. The Classical Tradition started with the *Historia Augusta* a century after Zenobia's death. Even if it is not as fantastic as the Arabic tradition, it is, however, open to various interpretations and susceptible to distortion[4]. Nevertheless, it became the main source on Zenobia and was adopted by other Graeco-Roman writers. Modern Western writers have provided a variety of serious studies based on excavations, inscriptions and research. The Arabic tradition, however, cannot be dismissed, for it indicates certain historical truths, although it ignored the relationship between Palmyra and the Roman Empire as if Rome had not been present in Syria. Rome is mentioned only twice in the history of Zenobia, by al-Ḳazwīnī and al-Ma'sūdī. Al-Ḳazwīnī reports that when al-Zabbā's father was killed by Djadhīma, king of the Tanūkh, she went to the Romans, recruited men, spent money and returned to her father's realm to drive Djadhīma away[5]. According to al-Ma'sūdī, 'Some say she [Zenobia] was Roman, but she spoke Arabic.[6]'

---

3. Al-Bounni, 1996.
4. Watson, 1998, 87.
5. Al-Ḳazwīnī, *Āthār al-Bilād*, Vol. 15, 424.
6. Al-Ma'sūdī, *Murūdj*, Vol. 2, 19.

The reasons for such flagrant ignorance were due to the fact that the Arab historians who wrote from the beginning of the ninth century lived mainly in 'Iraq and were influenced by the 'Iraqi school of historical tradition which followed and copied fanatically anti-Roman Persian sources. The Arab accounts of Odainat and Zenobia did not mention Odainat's campaigns in which he was gloriously victorious over the Persians in Syria and Mesopotamia[7] because they blindly followed the Persian sources, which deliberately ignored and erased from memory Sapor's defeat and humiliation. Sapor himself recorded his victories and forgot his defeat in inscriptions carved on the cliffs near Persopolis dubbed by archaeologists his res restae, in which he enumerated his victories over Gordian III and his Praetorian Prefect Philip the Arab at the battle of Misikhe in 244, and his victory and capture of Valerian at Edessa sixteen years later in 260. The inscriptions do not mention his defeat at the hands of Odainat in two campaigns in 260 and 266. This complete blackout by Persian sources on Odainat, Zenobia and the kingdom of Palmyra was for national Persian reasons. It was unfortunately followed by Arab historians and was the main reason for Rome's elimination from Zenobia's history. Persian sources glorified Persian victories and the humiliations which they inflicted upon the Romans, especially in Syria. Thus, al-Ṭabarī reports the capture of Valerian as follows: 'Sapor besieged the Roman King Valerian in Antioch, captured him and carried him to Jundisapor.[8]'

---

7. Gagé, 1964, 150 and 345.
8. Al-Ṭabarī, *Ta'rikh al-Rusul*, Vol. 2, 261.

Arab historians also copied Christian Syriac sources on Graeco-Roman history in Syria, but in a very limited and brief fashion. Syriac sources, however, also followed Persian sources. In other words, Arab historians from the eighth century onwards had their histories coloured by Persia against Rome.

Thus, Zenobia's rule, Roman wars and struggle to create an Arab Empire, suffered a total blackout in the Arabic sources, which concentrated instead on her struggle with Djadhīma, king of the Tanūkh, as if Rome had never held any sway in Syria. The legends that went round the Arab tents were oral, carried from tribe to tribe and tent to tent. Inflated and augmented by various groups, they are full of anecdotes, poetry and proverbs. The poetry, sometimes by well-known later poets, was added in order to guarantee the tales' authenticity.

Both Eastern and Western traditions agreed, however, on Zenobia's beauty, if not on her wisdom. According to al-Ḳazwīnī, she was the most beautiful woman of her time, her hair pulled behind her to cover her when she walked. The Western tradition also speaks of her beauty, of her black eyes that sparkled with fire, black hair, and teeth so white that many thought she had pearls for teeth[9]. The Arabic tradition emphasises her thick body hair, hence her name al-Zabbā', and speaks of her physical endurance and her spirit of decision, her taste for military life and the hunt, contrary to the stereotype of the Oriental woman. Both traditions describe her taste for luxury, and royal magnificence: she

---

9.　Al-Ḳazwīnī, *Āthār al-Bilād*, Vol. 15, 424; Hadas, 1958, 135.

was saluted with bowing in the Persian fashion. Her table followed the royal Persian style and included cups inserted with precious stones, but to the army she appeared in the Roman fashion, with a casque and a purple coat fringed with pearls[10]. Her court comprised eunuchs and nubile girls[11]. According to the Western tradition, she was chaste and virtuous and did not frequent her husband except to breed. In the Arabic tradition she was known not to care for men. The *Historia Augusta* attributes to her the victories of Odainat[12]. The Arabic tradition describes her as tricky, but also as the ablest of women[13].

Whilst Will describes her as a 'heroine of an unequal combat, and symbol of feminine emancipation'[14], Février emphasises her ferocious, insatiable ambition coupled with her underestimation of the enemy, and wonders whether she was reasonable to have challenged the masters of Rome[15].

Zenobia bears various names in Arab histories. Besides al-Zabbā, she is Naila, Layla, Maysūn, and Tadmur – the name of her city. She had a sister called Zubayba, who lived in a fort on the western side of the Euphrates, where Zenobia wintered, returning to Tadmur in the spring. Zenobia's story is mainly told by al-Ṭabarī (839–923) and followed with few variations by Ibn Khaldūn, Ibn al-Faḳīh,

---

10. Will, 1992, 190.
11. Starcky and Gawlikowski, 1985, 68.
12. Kotula, 1997, 124.
13. Al-Ḳazwīnī, *Āthār al-Bilād*, Vol. 15, 252.
14. Will, 1992, 198.
15. Février, 1931, 190.

al-Ma'sūdī[16], al-Ya'ḳūbī, Ibn al-Athīr, al-Ḳazwīnī and al-Iṣfahānī[17]. The story is briefly as follows.

Zenobia's father 'Umar b. Ḍarb was king of the Arabs of northern Syria. His army brought together the ancient tribe of 'Âd, Banū Saleh, Banu Halwan and Banū Ghara (the tribe of the royal dynasty of Edessa, the Abgharids) and Ḳuda'a. In his struggle against Djadhīma, king of the Tanūkh, for the control of the two banks of the Euphrates, 'Umar b. Ḍarb was defeated and killed. Zenobia, who succeeded him, promised revenge. She prepared for war, but her sister Zubayba warned her against a war of which the results were not certain, and advised her instead to fight Djadhīma by ruse. Zenobia agreed and wrote to Djadhīma offering marriage, since he was the only man worthy of her, and thus their two kingdoms would be united. Djadhīma was tempted. Nevertheless, he asked for the opinion of his friends, who all agreed except for one Ḳusair, who suggested that Djadhīma should ask her to come to him. If she accepted, she would be sincere; if not, Djadhīma would fall into her snare. Djadhīma ignored the suggestion and followed the advice of his nephew 'Umar b. 'Adī who encouraged Djadhīma by saying that his own tribe, the Namara, was allied with Zenobia, but that it would gladly obey Djadhīma in case of marriage.

Djadhīma prepared to go to her with his notables, and left his nephew in charge of his kingdom. Zenobia sent an

---

16. Al-Ma'sūdī, *Murūdj*, Vol. 2, 19; Ibn Khaldūn, *Ta'rikh*, Vol. 2, 259.

17. Al-Ṭabarī, *Ta'rikh al-Rusul*, Vol. 1, 365; al-Ḳazwīnī, *Āthār al-Bilād*, Vol. 15, 425; al-Ya'ḳūbī, *al-Kāmil*, Vol. 1, 209; Ibn al-Athīr, *al-Kāmil*, Vol. 1, 344; Ibn Khaldūn, *Ta'rikh*, Vol. 2, 270.

embassy with gifts to welcome him, but Ḳusair was suspicious and warned him again. Djadhīma persisted until he was brought into her presence. Zenobia received him lying in bed and lifted her skirt. Djadhīma was stunned by her thick body hair and realised too late that he had fallen into a trap. She asked him: 'What kind of bride do you see?' and he answered that one with such an appearance was not a suitable bride for him and that she was a maid without any shame! She placed him on a leather blanket, and asked him 'What kind of death would you like?' and he answered: 'An honourable death, that of a king'. She gave him a meal with plenty of wine until he began to doze, she then brought a golden basin and opened the veins of his wrists so that blood flowed into the basin – for the blood of kings heals madness. When some drops fell onto the floor she cried: 'Don't lose the blood of the king', and he feebly answered: 'The blood has been lost by its own!' Djadhīma bled to death and his companions returned crestfallen as her cavalry had encircled the palace. Ḳusair went to plead with 'Umar b. 'Adī for revenge, and 'Umar answered: 'How can I fight al-Zabbā', when she is stronger than an eagle?'

Zenobia expected and awaited revenge and went to consult several kāhins (priests and seers). One kāhina told her: 'Your destruction will come at the hands of 'Umar b. 'Adī, but your death is in your own hands.' Zenobia prepared for the worst, she dug a tunnel underneath her palace to a fort at the end of the town, and sent the best painter in the country to mix incognito in the circle of 'Umar b. 'Adī, and to paint him standing, riding, and with all his arms, so that she would be able to recognise him, for she had never set eyes on him.

Meanwhile, Ḳusair, desperate for a reaction which was not forthcoming from 'Umar b. 'Adī, planned for revenge. He mutilated his nose (immortalised by the proverb 'For some reason Kusair has cut his nose') and went to Zenobia, pretending to be a renegade and claiming that 'Umar b. 'Adī had flogged and mutilated him because he had advised Djadhīma to marry her. He remained with her until he gained her confidence, and told her he wished to go clandestinely to Iraq to bring her a caravan of treasures he had left behind – silk, perfumes and jewellery. She agreed. In Ḥīra he explained his plan to 'Umar b. 'Adī, and asked him for expensive merchandise. Zenobia liked what he brought, and sent him back for more, giving him a caravan of goods to sell in Iraq and bring it back loaded with luxuries. This was repeated, but on the third round Ḳusair asked 'Umar b. 'Adī for soldiers, two men replacing merchandise in boxes instead of saddle bags on each camel. 'Umar readily agreed to follow and Ḳusair briefed him on the tunnel where Zenobia would try to escape. Ḳusair preceded the caravan and went to Zenobia with the good news of its impending arrival, and asked her to come up to the roof to see for herself. To her surprise she saw the camels dragging their heavy loads to the ground. She turned tó Ḳusair and uttered her famous line:

'*Why are the camels proceeding so slow,*
Is it iron they carry, or men, to and fro?'

The caravan entered the city gates and as the last camel passed, the Nabatean doorkeeper, who was intrigued by the camels dragging along so slowly, poked his spear into the box, which touched the belly of the man inside who made wind. The doorman, alarmed, said in Nabatean *Beshta Beska*, this meaning that there was evil in the saddle bags.

The caravan alighted in the centre of the city, but the soldiers waited until dark, before they jumped from their boxes and massacred the garrison. The townsmen were not armed, and the city fell. Zenobia fled to the door of the tunnel where she recognised 'Umar b. 'Adī from the paintings, waiting for her. She immediately sucked her poisoned ring, saying: 'By my hand [I die] 'Umar, and not by yours.' 'Umar finished her with his sword and after destroying the town and taking the men as slaves, he returned to Iraq[18].

Djadhīma and his successor, 'Umar b. 'Adī, fare better in the Arab chronicles than Zenobia. This may be due to the fact that they used Arabic as the official language and not Aramaic as the other Arab principalities that preceded them, and that the legends gathered momentum when the Tanūkh replaced Palmyra in lording over the desert. Zenobia's glory had passed and her city was dead.

Djadhīma, a historical figure who is mentioned in an inscription at Umm al-Djimāl, ruled the Tanūkh for twelve years. He belonged to the Banu Zahran tribe from the 'Uzd. His ancestor, al-Raba'ī b. Nasr al-Lakhmi from Yaman, had a bad dream and called on the two famous *kāhins* Shaḳ and Satiḥ for an explanation. Their verdict was that he must emigrate immediately from Yaman. He then asked the

---

18. Millar, 1996, 433; Sartre, 2001, 987.

Persian King Yazdagird for permission to settle with his tribe on his territory. The king granted him settlement in Ḥīra (in Iraq) and gave him authority over the Arab tribes in the area. The conflict with 'Umar b. Ḍarb whose rule extended to the eastern bank of the Euphrates, ended with the defeat and death of Zenobia's father. She, in turn, tricked Djadhīma to his death[19]. This version of events in Arab chronicles was probably true, and Djadhīma's death may have been due to a defeat by the Palmyrans. According to al-Ṭabarī, one of the best Arab kings to have established a kingdom between Ḥīra and al-Anbar in Iraq, Djadhīma was known for his courage and wisdom. He received delegations and collected taxes. He was the first to wear shoes and had candles lit for him[20].

He professed to be a *kāhin* and claimed to be a prophet[21]. The conflict between the Tanūkh after their arrival in the area after 224, and the Palmyrans, was acute as the former counterbalanced Palmyra and aspired to take the latter's place as the only important Arab kingdom whose dominance was accepted by the Arab tribes. The Tanūkh resisted Zenobia's claim to control parts of the Roman Empire which were ruled by her husband in the Syrian desert and Arabia, and started to exercise power over the Arab tribes along the Euphrates and on the borders of Syria and Central Arabia[22].

---

19. Ibn Khaldūn, *Ta'rikh*, Vol. 2, 261.
20. Ibn Khaldūn (*Ta'rikh*, Vol. 2, 261), quotes al-Ṭabarī, *Ta'rikh al-Rusul*, Vol. 1.
21. Ibn Khaldūn, *Ta'rikh*, Vol. 2, 260; al-Ma'sūdī, *Murūdj*, Vol. 2, 20.
22. Dussaud, 1955, 66; Bowersock, 1983, 61, 136 and 137.

'Umar b. 'Adī b. Nasr b. Rabā'a, b. al-Ḥarith b. 'Umar b. Ghāra b. Lakhīm[23] who succeeded Djadhīma, made Ḥīra his capital. His son, Imru al-Ḳays, the first king of al-Nasr to be Christianised, and his grandson al-Nu'man b. el-Muntar would be the most famous member of the Lakhmid dynasty. It is interesting to compare Zenobia's genealogy in the Eastern and Western traditions. As the daughter of 'Umar b. Ḍarb, king of the Arabs, Zenobia had a pedigree harking back to Adam. She was distantly related to her husband Odainat since both had as common ancestors al-Nasr of Ḥira (called Nasôr in Palmyra), and further back in time, they shared an ancestor who descended from Adam, Ḥawbar al-'Amālīk, from the most ancient Arab (al-'Arāb) who is La'iṭ b. Sin b. Nu'a (Adam)[24].

In the Western sources, her descent is variously attributed to the pharaohs of Egypt[25], or to Antiochus IV, king of Syria (175–163 BC) and his wife Cleopatra, daughter of Ptotemy IV of Egypt[26]. On a bilingual inscription in Greek and Palmyran, discovered west of Palmyra on the road to Emesa on a milestone, she is described as Beth-Zabbâ, daughter of Antiochus[27]. The *Historia Augusta* calls her father Achilleo[28]. It has also been suggested that her father was Julius Aurelius Zenobios, *strategos* of Palmyra when Alexander Severus visited this colony with his army. This

23. Al-Ṭabarī, *Ta'rikh al-Rusul*, Vol. 1, 450.
24. Al-Ṭabarī, *Ta'rikh al-Rusul*, Vol. 1, 364.
25. Gibbon, 1934, 260.
26. Stoneman, 1992, 112.
27. Will, 1992, 187; Kotula, 1997, 116.
28. 'Alī, 1968–73, 107.

name is inscribed beneath a statue facing that of Zenobia and dates to 242[29].

It is beyond doubt that Zenobia was an Arab related to her husband Odainat. Her Aramaic name, Beth-Zabbâ, means 'daughter of Zabbaï' or 'Zabbaï' and is paralleled by her Arabic name al-Zabbâ. As to the Hellenistic names given to her supposed father, it was common for Greek names to be borne in Hellenised Palmyra.

Fantastic and sometimes unreal as Arabic legends and traditions on Zenobia and her time may seem, it is not true that they are devoid of any historical value, as some claim[30]. They confirm Zenobia's bid for supremacy among her Arab neighbours through her struggle with Djadhīma and 'Umar b. 'Adī[31] and her ambitious drive for an Arab empire based on the loyal Arab tribes that formed the bulk of her army, which challenged and defeated Rome.

Arabic sources describe Zenobia building a fort on the western bank of the Euphrates[32] and cities on both its eastern and western banks. She actually did build a city on the Euphrates called Zenobia for trade crossing the Euphrates and as a rival to the Persian Vologesias built by the Parthians in AD 60. In 540, the Persians captured the city of Zenobia and destroyed it. Justinian reconquered and rebuilt it. It was destroyed again by the Persians in 610.

---

29. Ingholt, 1976, 122 and 135; Sartre, 2001, 979, n. 107.
30. Homo, 1904, 89.
31. Stoneman, 1992, 11.
32. 'Alī (1968–73, 131–2), quotes al-Ṭabarī, Ta'rikh al-Rusul, Vol. 1, 32; al-Ma'sūdī, Murūdj, Vol. 2; al-Bakri, al-Masālik; and Yāḳūt, Mujam al-Buldan, Vol. 2.

Arabic tradition records Zenobia building a secret tunnel which ran under the walls of Tadmur to her sister's fort on the Euphrates[33].

Zenobia's suicide in the Arabic sources confirms the version provided by Zosimus in the Western historical tradition, although the methods were different – by poison according to the Arabic tradition, as opposed to starvation according to Zosimus. All, however, point to her erudition and eloquence. Arabic poetry and proverbs are attributed to her, and her erudition in Greek philosophy and literature features largely in the Western sources. The context, however, of her rise and fall in each tradition are worlds apart.

Zenobia's continued sway over Arab imagination and feelings across the centuries is best illustrated in Yāķūt and Ibn al-Faķīh[34] who reported that centuries after the fall and ruin of Palmyra, Marwān b. Muḥammad, the last Umayyad caliph, destroyed the remaining stretch of fortification of the city which by then was no larger than a village, and massacred its population which had disobeyed him and risen in revolt. During the destruction of the city, Marwān's men came upon a chasm in which was a nearly intact plastered house as if it had been only recently coated. Inside the house, the mummified body of a woman lay on her back with seventy robes and seven plaits of hair, but no toes. In her plaited hair was a golden plate thus inscribed: 'In the name of Allāh, I am Tadmur b. Haṣan, may Allāh

---

33. 'Alī, 1968–73, 133–4.
34. Yāķūt, *Mujam al-Buldan*, Vol. 2, 17; Ibn al-Faķīh, *Kitāb al-Buldan*, 115

grant shame on whoever enters my house.' The caliph took note, and ordered the house closed and the jewels left untouched. A few days later, he was killed.

The story links the discovery of an underground tomb with the superstitious fear of the curse of the dead. In fact the caliph did not die immediately from Zenobia's curse as the story would have us believe.

This story, however, is based on some historical facts. Zenobia's wall, rebuilt and strengthened by Emperor Diocletian (284–305) and subsequently added to and repaired by Emperor Justinian (527–65), was intact at the time of the Arab Conquest. Thus it remained under the Rashīdin caliphate and the Umayyads, until it was destroyed by Marwān II. The house-tomb adjacent to the wall, rock-carved and closed by a boulder instead of a door, is similar to another tomb (Ben Noimo) recently excavated, which was devoid of a door but closed by a stone slab. The 'bed' mentioned in Arabic sources was in fact the funerary couch. As to the curse, similar inscriptions have been found in a few other tombs. Yākūt associated Marwān's assassination and final defeat with the curse: this belief was widespread in the Middle Ages, and is still adhered to by some writers even now[35].

The ruins of Palmyra inspired poets who roamed nostalgically amongst them. Muhammad al-Tamīmi (806–45) came upon two beautiful girls carved in relief, probably on a tombstone:

---

35. Al-Bounni, 1972 73–6.

'Tell me maids of Tadmur
Are you not bored with your long stay
As on silent marble you lay
How many nights have you passed
Since the years and the night that was your last?'

Another poet, Abū Dalaf, in the mid-tenth century, fell under the spell of a relief on another tombstone (Fig. 22):

'Maids of Tadmur, you have pierced my heart.
Sleep vanishes when I think of you.
Are you not bored with the familiarity of the eternal
embrace?
If only time could throw between you the sword of
parting.'

And the poet Abū 'l-Ḥaṣan al-Arīlalī recorded:

'I saw two statues in Tadmur and I ask whether
beautiful pictures are not afraid of the passage of
time.'[36]

---

36. Free translation based on Yāḳūt, *Mujam al-Buldan*, Vol. 2, 18 and Ibn al-Faḳīh, *Kitāb al-Buldan*, 110–11.

CHAPTER VIII

Zenobia's Tadmur

Tadmur, an ancient Semitic foundation, a station between the Euphrates and the Mediterranean, was known in the second millennium BC. It was peopled by two ethnic waves from Arabia – the Canaanites and Amorites. These were followed by the Aramaeans who settled in the oasis around 1100 BC[1] and later by waves of Arab tribes who gave it its Arab complexion.

In the nineteenth century BC, an Assyrian contract in Cappadocia mentions as a witness 'Ishtar the Tadmurian'. In the eighteenth century BC, two cuneiform letters from Mari mention Tadmur. At the beginning of the eleventh century BC, the annals of Tiglath Pilasar refer to Tadmur as being in the country of Amurru[2]. When the East was divided in the fourth century BC after the death of Alexander the Great, the Seleucids in Syria and Ptolemies in Egypt and Palestine clashed frequently. At the Battle of Raphia, the Egyptian Pharaoh Ptolemy IV defeated the Seleucid King Antiochus VI. The latter had the support of the Arab Shaykh Zabadibêlos, who was probably Palmyran (since his

---

1. Starcky, 1960, 1078; Shahîd, 1984a, 38.
2. Al-Bounni and al-As'ad, 1987, 14 and 16.

name is known only in Palmyra[3]) at the head of ten thousand Arabs. In the second century BC, the Seleucids took Palestine and Phoenicia from the Ptolemies and promoted Hellenisation. In the first century, Palmyra was an independent city[4] which soon became an important centre. A century later, Palmyra and its territory constituted an Arab principality, similar to Petra, Emesa and Iturea, and became a station for caravans, with a highly efficient corps of desert police. After the collapse of the Seleucid empire in AD 64, Pompey conquered Syria, including Tadmur, which remained autonomous and grew rich owing to the increase of trade under Roman rule. The triumvir Mark Anthony, after his debacle with the Parthians, sent word to Tadmur in 41 BC saying he wanted to rest his soldiers in the city and organised a raid on the town to fill his caskets, but the inhabitants fled with their treasure beyond the Euphrates, and Mark Anthony found an empty town. Palmyra was then a buffer state enjoying certain privileges with the two great empires[5]. Surrounded on their borders by Romans and Parthians, the Palmyrans were merchants who assured the movement of goods from the East via the Persian Gulf to the West (Fig. 24). They had good relations with the Parthians who allowed them to have trading posts on the Euphrates, at Vologesias, Ctesiphon, Seleucia, Spasinou Charax and Phorath[6]. Palmyra was now in the Roman

---

3. Starcky, 1960, 1079.
4. Dunant, 1983, 140.
5. Starcky, 1960, 1079; Jones, 1971, 265; Browning, 1979, 23.
6. Sartre-Fauriat, 1997, 259.

sphere, and in the reign of Tiberius, the governor of Syria in AD 11–17 delineated the borders of Palmyra[7]. It was then that the name of Palmyra was first mentioned, the settlement having been known until then as Tadmur (Fig. 25)[8]. It was integrated into the Province of Syria probably around AD 17–19, during Germanicus' mission to Syria. From then onwards, a Roman garrison was stationed in Palmyra which, moreover, furnished auxiliary troops of archers and dromedaries to the Roman army[9]. Despite its annexation by Rome, it retained a larger degree of independence than was allowed to any other provincial city[10].

The city was a federation of clans, of which twenty-five are known. Four held a privileged position, Bene Mattabôl, Bene Mâzin, Bene Zaydbôl and Bene Kamâra. These four tribes were not primitive tribes that had given birth to Palmyra, but were new civic divisions introduced in the Imperial period. They may date to Hadrian's reign[11]. With a Semitic basis and a growing proportion of partially Hellenised Arab tribes, the city was governed by the Senate, the people's assembly (*demos*), annual magistrates (*archontes*) and the four tribes until AD 260[12]. Thus, with its local institutions, Palmyra was Republican until the advent

---

7.   Colledge, 1976b, 50; al-Bounni and al-As'ad, 1987, 18.
8.   Jones, 1971, 265; Colledge, 1976b, 47 and 50.
9.   Kotula, 1997, 90.
10. Jones, 1971, 266.
11. Al-As'ad and Gawlikowski, 1986–7, 11; Rey-Coquais, 1978, 51.
12. Gagé, 1964, 142.

of Odainat and resembled other Greek cities of the Roman Empire, except for the predominant roles of the four tribes and an administration more independent than in other cities. Custom duties were not collected by the Roman State, and taxes on merchandise belonged to the city, but it is probable that the imperial treasury had some rights on custom duties. Palmyra's status in relation to Rome did not resemble that of other provinces, the name of the emperor was not struck on the coins of the city and, while Rome only allowed the use of Latin and Greek – the two official languages of the empire –, Palmyra did not submit to this rule for it used Aramaic, the language used in Syria and Palestine. Palmyran soldiers who died in Britain and Africa, were given Palmyran epitaphs. The names of the months were not the Macedonian ones which officials used in Syria, but those used in the countryside and by the Arab tribes. These names are of unknown origin and, although they appear in Assyrian cuneiform, they are not Assyrian, and were used wherever Aramaic was spoken[13]. They are used in Syria even today.

Owing to its exceptional position and its local militia of famous archers, Palmyra controlled the desert between Emesa and the Euphrates and ensured security. It developed the infrastructure necessary for military enterprises beyond its borders and facilitated the passage of the Romans across the desert wastes. The Roman outpost of Dura-Europos could not have existed without Palmyra[14]. The support of

---

13. Mommsen, 1985, 798–9, n. 4.
14. Sartre, 1991, 335–6; Bowersock, 1983, 29.

Palmyran soldiers was useful to Roman soldiers in Syria and Arabia, and for the campaigns of Trajan, Lucius Verus, Avidius Cassius, Septimius Severus and Alexander Severus against Parthia. Palmyra provided archers, heavy cavalry and supplies and it was probably the base of operations[15]. Palmyra was visited by Hadrian in AD 129, a visit lavishly financed by a certain merchant called Agrippa. The emperor gave Palmyra the title of *Hadriana* and declared it a free city, relinquishing to the people's assembly and to the Senate the right to set and collect taxes. Financial control was no longer in the hands of the provincial governor in Antioch, but held by a curator appointed by the emperor[16], and the city was given dispensation from furnishing lodgings for troops[17]. Palmyra's status changed when it became a colony and, in 212, Palmyrans became Roman citizens. The honour of being a Roman citizen included obligations, such as municipal duties and funding public monuments and administration. The city's status changed again with the rise of the dynasty of Odainat under the patronage of Rome, but remained distinct from that of client states like Nabatea and Osrhoene.

Odainat's family received favours from the Severans and Philip the Arab. Emperor Valerian followed suit by appointing Odainat governor of Phoenicia. Meanwhile, Sapor occupied Armenia in 252–3 and besieged Edessa. Intent on relieving Edessa, Valerian entered it under siege,

---

15. Février, 1931, 64.
16. Al-Bounni and al-As'ad, 1987, 20.
17. Teixidor, 1984, 91.

but there was no food in the city and he was afraid of a mutiny. He therefore opened negotiations with Sapor which ended in Valerian's treacherous capture by the Persians. Antioch, the capital of Syria, fell to the Persians for the first time through a traitor Márédés, a rich citizen banished by the Council for embezzling public funds. Surprised by the invader, the inhabitants offered no resistance, the town was pillaged and its treasures taken. Sapor finally killed the traitor for an unknown reason. Some historians say he had proclaimed himself emperor[18]. Palmyra, from the beginning, was ambivalent in her political allegiances to East and West. Every time war broke out, the question was raised as to which side Palmyra would take[19], and, although the Palmyrans were part of the Roman world, they looked towards the East. Palmyra is sometimes described as an outpost of the Parthian East, close to Hatra which developed as a religious centre for the Arab population of the desert. In this climate of disintegration, it was natural for Odainat to turn to the East[20] and throw in his lot with Persia, although this ended in a rebuff which obliged him to reverse his opinion and turn to Rome.

Palmyran Commerce: the Caravan Trade

In turning to the East, Odainat attempted to protect Palmyra's commerce, the source of its wealth. Its prosperity harked back to the break-up of the Seleucid Empire, when

18. Mommsen, 1985, 808.
19. Mommsen, 1985, 796.
20. Mare, 1995, 203.

commerce was disrupted, the Arab tribes captured the trade, and Tadmur, the principal oasis in the Syrian desert, rose to importance thanks to revenues from goods in transit and dues for drawing water from its spring[21]. The first stage of its prosperity corresponds to the Hellenistic period, but Palmyra flourished under Rome in the second and third centuries AD, during which time most of its public buildings were erected. Besides transiting commerce which Palmyran caravans carried, Palmyra traded in salt from the rich salt mines near the city and participated in the importation of Asiatic slaves into the Roman Empire. Palmyra also traded in purple cloths manufactured in Neapolis and Lydda, henna, and salted fish from Lake Tiberias in Palestine[22], in medicinal items, kitchen spices, ornaments and home decoration[23]. It also traded in Chinese silk which was subsequently coloured and mixed with other textiles in the workshops of Beirut and Tyre. Silk became very popular in Rome after Emperor Elagabalus started sporting clothes entirely of silk. Jewellery too was an important item of trade, as Palmyra had corporations of workers in gold and silver[24]. To regulate commercial law and taxes, the old and new financial laws and taxes, as well as dues on all goods in transit, were inscribed in Aramaic and Greek on a 'tariff stone', dated to AD 137 and now in the Hermitage Museum in St Petersburg. Almost all the commerce with the Orient

---

21. Jones, 1971, 265.
22. Février, 1931, 48, 49 and 61.
23. Mare, 1995, 203 and 211.
24. Mommsen, 1985, 800.

and Far East was brought by caravans through the Persian Gulf. Roman roads which had originally been built for strategic reasons profited Palmyran commerce, as did the Palmyran colonies in Vologesias, Charax and Phorath. Egypt traded with the Far East through Palmyran merchants who had settled in Alexandria. Palmyra's *raison d'être* was commerce. The zenith of its economic and cultural activity was reached in the third century, after it had inherited Petra's commerce which declined after Petra's annexation by Trajan. Palmyra retained business links with the Nabateans, of whom many served in the Palmyran army in the second century[25].

Rome profited from Palmyra's commercial activity and its supervision of the Beduins and caravans, and Palmyra profited for more than a century from relative peace.

The caravans had begun as tribal or family enterprises. The desert chieftains became caravan merchants, and the caravan merchants soon became sea merchants controlling river-borne transport on rafts to the ports of the Kingdom of Mesene which had links with the Kushan Empire in the Indus valley[26]. The caravans connected the centres which imported products from regions further east, and through the shipping business imported goods from India and China[27]. The caravans developed into a huge enterprise. Their organisers had to be wealthy – bankers as well as merchants – in order to provide food for men and animals,

---

25. Février, 1931, 58.
26. Gawlikowski, 1995, 2 and 4–5.
27. Mattingly, 1995, 227.

camels and horses, equipment and means of protection with archers as escorts. Horses for the caravans were bred in the mountainous zone north-west of Palmyra and the breeding of camels took place in the desert, where the great merchant families kept their links with the nomadic tribes[28]. The merchants became rich, especially with the luxury commerce of perfumes from the East, pearls, incense and myrrh from Arabia, and they played the traditional role of benefactors, building monuments in Palmyra.

The itinerary followed by the caravans joined Palmyra to Vologesias, Ctesiphon, Phorath and Spasinu Charax, and the round trip of 1,200km took a month (Fig. 15). Palmyran merchants who had settled in these cities received the merchandise and stored it in warehouses in anticipation of the caravans. Goods in transit were kept in warehouses near Palmyra before being taken to Mediterranean ports[29].

The itinerary changed in the third century owing to the Sassanid occupation of the independent Arab state of Characne at the mouth of the Tigris and Euphrates. The routes were lengthened by a detour northwards through Nisibis, Edessa and Antioch[30].

Palmyra: the City

Just before the birth of Zenobia, the town of Palmyra underwent renovation on a monumental scale under the Severan dynasty, particularly Alexander Severus (222–35).

---

28. Van Berchem, 1976, 165.
29. Sartre-Fauriat, 1997, 266; Dunant, 1983, 143.
30. Dunant, 1983, 145.

In AD 250, with 150,000 inhabitants (some put it at 200,000), Palmyra was one of the largest towns of the empire[31]. In size it was comparable to Antioch; and Alexandria, the largest town in the Near East, was barely twice as large[32]. Its aristocracy consisted of leaders of caravans, owners of camels and Persian Gulf merchants, and although for three centuries it was in the Roman zone of influence, Palmyra was not a typical Roman town. It had no gymnasium nor amphitheatre[33] but it did include baths, for the so-called Baths of Diocletian existed long before his time[34], and its streets were not paved to ease the passage of camels[35].

The town's inner wall, which included a series of towers and bastions, enclosed the principal civic structures of a residential area. This wall existed in the time of Odainat and Zenobia, but part of it was erected when Zenobia was faced with disaster. Built of unbaked bricks, it enclosed the gardens around the source of Efqa, but excluded the western quarter. In the first century AD, it fell out of use because of the town's extension, but the southern part remained in use and was again linked up to a new system of natural defence which used the crests and the ridges against nomads and mounted troops. A second, outer, wall was built in the middle of the second century after the

---

31. Kotula, 1997, 93.
32. Al-Bounni and al-As'ad, 1987, 72.
33. Stoneman, 1992, 67.
34. Al-Bounni, 1978, quoted by Ḥālak, 2002, 38.
35. Will, 1992, 125.

completion of the colonnaded street. An *agora* – a rectangle surrounded by a Corinthian portico on all four sides – was built in the second century in the reign of Hadrian. Two hundred statues graced the *agora*, each standing on the bracket of a column: statues of senators on the eastern side, of Palmyran officials on the northern side, of soldiers on the west and caravan leaders on the south. Its banquet chamber included an altar and shallow steps on three sides, used as couches for diners.

A colonnaded street, about 1,200m long, ran from east to west. Built after the completion of the temple of Bêl in the second century, it linked the *propylaeum* of the temple of Bêl with the monumental arch and was lined with porticos, each 7m wide (Fig. 27). Halfway up each column, the brackets for statues projected over the roadway. Those near the monumental arch were never endowed with statues, the project having been cut short by Aurelian (Fig. 28). Reminiscent of a triumphal arch of the Imperial period and integrated into the design of two streets, the monumental arch with three bays was built at the beginning of the third century. The theatre, a standard Roman model built in AD 200 in the Severan period (Figs. 31 and 32), was never completed[36]. A *Tetrapylon* stood at one of the centres of the city, off the main north colonnade (Figs. 29 and 30) as did a richly decorated *Nymphaeum* with a semi-circular water basin ornamented with bold reliefs.

---

36. Millar, 1996, 329. The theatre was excavated and partly reconstructed by K. al-As'ad. The wall of the stage is 45m long.

Partial excavations of the residential quarter, with its mesh of parallel streets to the west of the *Tetrapylon* have brought to light a particular type of Mediterranean house with a peristyle-court paved with mosaics exhibiting Hellenistic themes and style, geometric patterns, theatrical masks in relief and mythological figures, as in Antioch and other parts of Syria. External walls were generally devoid of windows – a typically Oriental characteristic[37]. It is of note that only 30 per cent of the surface of Palmyra has been excavated up until now.

Palmyrene Religion

Palmyran inscriptions mention twenty-two gods of whom the two chief gods were Bêl and Ba'alšamîn, identified with Zeus, and the twenty-two included the Canaanite group of Astarte, Reshef and Shadraba, as well as the local gods Yarhibôl (the Sun god), 'Aglibôl (the Moon god) and the Syrian goddess Atargatis. Early Palmyran religious beliefs bore Mesopotamian influence, depicting the gods Bêl and Nebu, and Mesopotamian myths (Figs. 33 and 34). Greek and Roman gods were absent, and only Nemesis, the goddess of destiny, was venerated. During the Hellenistic period, Arab penetration brought numerous new gods, Allât, Šams (the sun), Ba'alšamîn (of Canaanite origin and whose worship was introduced to Palmyra by Arab tribes), Raḥim, 'Azîzu, Abgal, Manât, Mâ'an and Arsu. Allât was identified with Athena and Manât with Nemesis. Like other

---

37. Will, 1992, 114; al-Bounni and al-Asᶜad, 1987, 93.

Arabs, the Palmyrans depicted their gods on horses and camels, and gave them the epithet 'Ra mîn' and 'Ra im'. Their cults reflected Arab rituals and beliefs: circumambulation, processions and animal sacrifices. They believed in *betyls* (stones representing the gods' abodes) and in the *ginnaya* (the good djinn). After Tadmur had been Christianised, its bishop was described at the Council of Antioch in 363 as the 'Bishop of the Arabs'[38]. In the first century, under Roman rule, sanctuaries and communion banqueting halls were constructed. A theological astral system was elaborated which incorporated current beliefs, but gradually a spiritual change took place in Palmyra, and the transcendental conception of the divine created an unknown god who was identified with Ba'alšamîn. In AD 200, a leading citizen of Palmyra who was president of the Senate had a dedication incised 'To God, one, unique and merciful'[39]. This tendency which consists in invoking God without naming him is Arab. The temples played a fundamental role in the city's social network. Rich Palmyrans left detailed wills in favour of sanctuaries to which they felt committed, endowing them lavishly[40]. The plan of the sanctuaries remained Semitic. The *cella*, the god's abode in the middle of a large square enclosure (*temenos*), contained a niche (*adyton*) for the cult image[41].

---

38. Al-Bounni, 1978, quoted by Ḥālak, 2002, 35.
39. Starcky and Gawlikowski, 1985, 101–2, 107 and 110.
40. Drijvers, 1995, 119; Dussaud, 1955, 98; Will, 1992, 105.
41. Starcky, 1960, 1099.

The Palmyran temple of Bêl, the first god of one of the
oldest Semitic pantheons, is comparable in its general
conception to the temples of Ebla and Ugarit, which are a
thousand years older[42]. It is unique and surprising with its
refined architecture in the Hellenistic tradition (Fig. 36) of
Antioch and its richness of decoration. It was erected by the
Roman government during the reign of Tiberius to impress
the Palmyrans, in an act of Roman propaganda to celebrate
perhaps the inclusion of Palmyra in Provincia Syria. It also
received contributions from Palmyrans living in Babylon
and in other trading centres. Construction began in AD 19
and the *cella* was inaugurated in AD 32, but it was not
completed until the middle of the second century. The
temple became the religious centre of all Palmyrans, and
represented all the sanctuaries in town[43]. Built on an
artificial tell on the site of an earlier structure – probably
Sumerian or Babylonian – as a political gesture financed by
Rome which also sent masons, it is the work of a great
master. Artists and architects must have hailed from
religious centres such as Hierapolis, which followed the
Hellenistic tradition, but the actual layout of the temple is
Semitic[44]. It comprised a large court 200 m long, with an
arcaded banqueting hall in Mesopotamian style and a
maintenance workshop permanently attached to the
sanctuary[45]. Built of stone in a mudbrick town with bronze

---

42. Stoneman, 1992, 65.
43. Drijvers, 1995, 119.
44. Colledge, 1976a, 48–52.
45. Will, 1995, 29, 34 and 35.

Ionic capitals and fluted columns, it dominated the town. The *adyton* in the *cella*, the holy of holies which preserves the divine presence from profane contact, is characteristic of Semitic piety. In Graeco-Roman temples, the image of the divinity stood in the main niche, accessible to all. The *cella* included two inner sanctuaries, the northern and southern *adyta*, one for the images of the trinity, Bêl, Yarhibôl (Sun god) and 'Aglibôl (Moon god), the other for the objects carried in the procession, probably a portable idol and Bêl's bed[46].

The *propylaea* were swept away in 1132. They comprised two staircases which rose to the roof, a colossal door and ramp for the sacrificial animals (camels, bulls and rams but not swine) that were led into the *temenos*, a sacred basin – a rectangular tank at the entrance of the temple where the priests symbolically washed themselves – and the temple's utensils. The ceiling of the *adyton* (Fig. 37) consisted of a simple slab of stones with a carved cupola adorned with the signs of the seven planets, Jupiter in the centre surrounded by the twelve signs of the zodiac (Fig. 38), and at the four corners the spread eagle of Jupiter in a star-studded sky. High crossbeams supported the ceiling of the Peristyle and in a remaining fragment of the second beam a characteristically Arab rite is carved in relief: a camel bearing on its back a high pavilion of brilliant red leather, which covered the *betyl* (Fig. 39) The guardian of the tabernacle follows on a horse or a donkey. Veiled women

---

46. Starcky, 1960, 1088; Will, 1992, 138–9; Kaizer, 2002, 67.

accompany the procession (Fig. 40) which poses in front of four persons raising their right hands in a salutation or benediction. The scene could be interpreted as the foundation of the sanctuary[47]. Others interpret the procession as the arrival of the goddess Allât in Palmyra, brought by the tribe of Bene Mâzin, or as the procession which enthroned the *betyl* in the temples of Bêl. *Betyls* were stones embodying the divinities venerated by the Arabs in pre-Islamic times[48]. The temple was run by a college of powerful priests presided over by a symposiarch, the highest religious figure in Palmyra. None outside the circle formed by the merchant aristocracy was admitted to their gathering (*thiase*). The wealth of the temple attests to the profits made in the caravan-trade.

The temple of the Lord of Heaven, Ba'alšamîn, rivalled the temple of Bêl, and was also dedicated to 'Aglibôl and Malakbôl, who with Ba'alšamîn formed another trinity venerated by Arab tribes (Figs. 41 and 42). The temple is dated to ca AD 130–1. Ba'alsamîn, *marê-'alma* ('Master of the World') was identified with 'Zeus most high who hears', a supreme god but closer to human beings and identified with the anonymous god. An altar in front of the *cella* was dedicated to 'Zeus most high who hears' and does not mention the name Ba'alšamîn but does mention an unnamed god. Other inscriptions describe him as 'great and merciful' (*ra mâna*). This anonymity marks an evolution in

<hr>

47. Al-Bounni and As'ad, 1987, 50.
48. This interpretation is contested. See Drijvers, 1995, 119; Starcky, 1960, 1099; Drijvers, 1995, 119.

the piety of the Palmyrans towards a more spiritual worship – attested by the incense altars dedicated 'to him whose name is blessed for ever, good and merciful'[49]. The thesis that the anonymous god is identified with Ba'alšamîn is doubted by some, as only one of the altars with the above inscription was found in his temple[50].

At the gathering of the sacred company of priests (*marze a* in Palmyran or *thiase* in Greek) in the temple of Ba'alšamîn in an independent chapel, admission was by ticket in the form of a terracotta tessera bearing the symbol or the image of the god honoured and for whose feast worshippers gathered[51]. A bath for ritual washing was taken before the meal. The priests ate, reclining on couches, and wine was drunk in a kind of 'eucharist', since the god also was present at this communion feast (Figs. 43, 44 and 45).

The temple of Allât was located outside the walls of Palmyra. In AD 300, thirty years after the destruction of the city, it was incorporated in Diocletian's camp. It has recently been uncovered by the Polish Archaeological Mission. Allât, the warrior goddess of the Arabs, is identified with Athena and Atargatis[52] accompanied by her animal the lion, and also with Artemis 'lady of the wild beasts'. The Bene Mâzin, one of the four tribes of Palmyra, brought the cults of Ba'alšamîn and Allât to Palmyra, thus explaining the

---

49. Starcky, 1960, 1098; Stoneman, 1992, 71.
50. Dussaud, 1955, 115; al-Bounni and al-As'ad, 1987, 61; Kaizer, 2002, 160.
51. Stoneman, 1992, 73.
52. Dussaud, 1955, 90.

marked resemblance between the two temples. Both shrines were transformed into Graeco-Roman temples in the second century AD.[53] The Bene Mâzin were responsible for the temple of Allât and of two deities associated with her, Rahim and sams – both named on a console of the colonnade on the edge of the camp. Dated to the middle of the second century, the *cella* exhibits eighty inscriptions and graffiti, of which some are in Safaitic. A lion with an oryx between his legs and the inscription 'Allât to bless anyone who will not shed blood in this temple' which has been dated between 103 BC and AD 64, probably stood at the gate of the temple and is now in the museum of Palmyra. The temple includes a courtyard and a peristyle of fluted columns[54].

The temple of Nebu, son of Bêl-Marduk – the Mesopotamian god of art and science, and the scribe of the tables of destiny who was popular in Palmyra – was constructed in the first century AD with a contribution from the family of Elahbêl known for building the most beautiful of the tower-tombs (Figs. 51 and 52). It stood on a podium surrounded by thirty-two Corinthian columns. The *propylaeum* was in the form of a six-column vestibule, with a majestic stairway at the southern end.

The temples of Ba'alšamin, Allât and Nebu illustrate the local architectural tradition which leaned heavily on Parthian art[55].

---

53. Drijvers, 1995, 116.
54. Al-Bounni and al-As'ad, 1987, 68; Drijvers, 1995, 109–10 and 115; Kaizer, 2002, 170.
55. Al-Bounni and al-As'ad, 1987, 59.

The temple of Bêlhammûn was a high place dedicated to the Phoenician-Canaanite god Bêlhammûn associated on some inscriptions with the Arab goddess of Fate (Manât), who is identified with Nemesis[56].

The temple of Arsu, a major Arab god, has been recently excavated. It was destroyed when Diocletian repaired Zenobia's wall at the end of the third century. A member of the tribe of Bene Mattabôl funded in AD 280 the restoration of its ceiling, seven years after the second destruction of Palmyra by Aurelian's soldiers[57].

The sites of other shrines are yet to be discovered and identified: those of Atargatis, of Sams, the Sacred Wood and the sanctuary of 'Aglibôl, the *Templum Solis* and the sanctuary of Malakbêl.

The Cult of the Dead

The Palmyrans had a consuming preoccupation with the afterlife (Figs. 46 and 47). The *naphša* (soul), sometimes considered as living in the sun, was symbolised by a stele. Bodies were sometimes mummified and, forming a link between the conservation and the survival of the soul, a tomb was called 'House of Eternity'[58].

The religious beliefs of the Greek world were known in Palmyra. The happy immortality of the soul is illustrated in frescoes in the *hypogeum* of the Three Brothers (Fig. 54). Achilles casting off the feminine garb under which he hid his

---

56. Al-Bounni and al-As'ad, 1987, 68–9.
57. Al-As'ad and Gawlikowski, 1986–7, 14–5.
58. Starcky and Gawlikowski, 1985, 1110.

identity at the court of the king of the Dolopes on the Greek island of Scyros symbolises the soul leaving the body for a better life – a belief based on Neoplatonic teaching. This theme from the Achilles cycle, which developed from the *Iliad* and emphasised the eternity of the soul, was not only depicted in tombs but also in Palmyran houses[59]. The need for the survival of body and soul is reflected in funerary banquets which indicate a desire to give the dead a little of the existence they lost.

Funerary banquets were held in temples, and the funerary meal included a cake of almonds, symbolising the afterlife[60]. In a tomb discovered by H. Ingholt, the ceiling was decorated with a brown, painted eagle. According to certain ancient theories, it is precisely this bird – the eagle – which carried the soul of the deceased to the sun[61].

The tomb (Bt Lm), 'House of Eternity', was the place where the dead enjoyed a form of survival and received honours from their descendants[62]. It stood as a visible

---

59. Achilles in the *gynaeceum* of the king of the Dolopes casting off his female disguise and heading for the Trojan War, was a popular theme of third-century AD mosaic pavements in the Eastern Mediterranean. This scene was notably depicted on the *triclinium* pavement of a wealthy villa in Neapolis (Nablūs) in Palestine dating to the reign of Emperor Philip the Arab (AD 244–9). See Dauphin, 1979, 12–14. More recently, it was discovered decorating the floor of a shallow pool in the second to mid-third century House of Poseidon at Seleucia Zeugma on the Euphrates in eastern Turkey (Önal, 2002, 22–6).
60. Starcky and Gawlikowski, 1985, 1110.
61. Al-Bounni and al-As'ad, 1987, 45.
62. Will, 1992, 117–8.

monument to the wealth and power of a family. Tower-tombs and temple-tombs were deliberately erected in the valley through which passed the caravans travelling between Palmyra and the Mediterranean[63]. There were three kinds of burial places in Palmyra: tower-tombs, house or temple-tombs, and underground tombs. The earliest were the tower-tombs, scattered on the hills surrounding Palmyra, similar to funerary towers found in other Arab towns, such as Hatra, Emesa and Edessa. Built in the early Hellenistic period on a steeply stepped base, tower-tombs consisted of several floors of interments reached by a narrow staircase, and with *loculi* on each landing into which the bodies of the dead were placed and sealed with a sculptured portrait of the deceased (Fig. 48). An arched recess decorated with vine enclosed the main funerary group with the head of the family lying on a couch, his wife at his feet and his sons standing behind him (Fig. 49). The couch was a cloth-wrapped mattress in a frame[64]. Children were mainly buried in rectangular grave-pits in the floor, but were mostly buried with the adults[65].

The four-storied tower-tomb of Jamblichus, dated to AD 83, was capped by a carved cornice (Figs. 47 and 50). The walls were internally lined with Corinthian pillars, between which were set tiers of *loculi*. The ceiling was decorated with a pattern of diamond and triangle-shaped coffers which contained portrait busts. The tomb of Elahbêl, dated to AD 103, had Corinthian pillars and a ceiling with

---

63. Al-Asʿad and Yon, 2001, 100–2.
64. Browning, 1979, 192–4; Will, 1992, 147.
65. Kiyohide, 1995, 21–6.

geometric coffers containing rosettes (Figs. 51 and 52). Each individual tomb was closed with a stone[66].

The Polish Mission has established that tower-tombs of the first century AD were erected above a *hypogeum* complex. In such tombs, the main door led by steps down to the subterranean *hypogeum*. Some tower-tombs were used for two hundred years and thus served many generations. *Hypogea* or house-tombs were underground galleries hewn into the rock on a cruciform plan. Common in the middle of the second century, they were the only type of sepulchre which lasted until the third quarter of the third century. Tower-tombs and *hypogea*, however, had become quite distinct in the first century. These were the tombs of rich merchants, priests, city officials and army commanders. Tower-tombs, however, were replaced in the middle of the second century by temple-tombs owing to a change in Palmyran taste under Graeco-Roman influence[67]. Common people were buried in small graves in the desert.

In the *hypogeum* of the Three Brothers, a T-shaped chamber with sixty-five recesses which accommodated several generations of the same family (Fig. 53), the barrel vault was painted with a pattern of hexagrams, a panel depicting the Hellenistic theme of the abduction of Ganymede and a series of frescoes in Greek-Syrian style (Fig. 54). Built in the early third century, this *hypogeum* blended Hellenistic and Oriental Parthian traditions[68].

---

66. Browning, 1979, 192–4.
67. Al-As'ad and Yon, 100.
68. Browning, 1979, 206, 209–10; Starcky, 1960, 1091.

Modest tombs consisted of a simple stele bearing the name or the image of the dead *naphša*. Such tombs were also known in Nabatea and south Arabia[69]. There were also burial clubs for the poor, with a subscription[70]. The number of *hypogea* increased in the second century. According to Gawlikowski, this marked the decline of patriarchal families and resulted from the growth of the middle class[71].

Tomb portraits were accompanied by the names of the deceased inscribed in Palmyran. In some cases, a veil was drawn over their features.

The tombs belonged to rich families, all of whose members joined in the expenses as a matter of one-upmanship in front of other Palmyrans[72]. Sometimes part of the *hypogea* was sold to relatives and friends, and more than one individual could own parts of the same tomb, a niche, or an exedra, in a kind of co-ownership. Inscriptions of cession, this including the sale of tombs, indicate that cession of a portion of a tomb was not restricted to family members. The sale transactions illustrate the role of women in society and indicate that they were entitled to manage their own properties, their husband's or their children's. Slave women, on being freed, formed a distinct social group (*bt ḥry*) and were also entitled to trade property as purchasers and sellers. Some documents, however, contain restrictions on inheritance rights, reserving it to male heirs

---

69. Starcky, 1960, 1088.
70. Stoneman, 1992, 68.
71. Gawlikowski, 1970, 182; Teixidor, 1984, 52.
72. Stoneman, 1992, 70.

only. Female heirs did not inherit property and were excluded from the rights of disposing of it, but they retained the right of being buried in the family tomb. Some texts contain a clause restricting burial to family members only. An inscription dated to AD 95 describes two women who jointly owned a tomb divided into two equal shares. An inscription records a transaction conducted by a woman acting in place of her husband, alive but absent[73].

Costume

Costumes, as depicted in reliefs and sculptures, bore witness to Parthian influence and consisted of a short tunic with long sleeves enhanced by gold braids from the shoulder to the wrist, a tunic and pantaloons (Fig. 55). On other tomb-reliefs the Greek dress is shown with short sleeves and a short, knee-length tunic. Women wore turbans and shawls on their heads, and much jewellery (Figs. 5, 6 and 7) – gold, silver and precious stones, as well as chains of pearls in their hair[74]. The local costume may have been that favoured by the Arab gods, 'Azîzu, Ma'an, Ša'ar and Abgâl on reliefs. Under the Romans, members of the middle class wore both Greek and Parthian clothes[75].

The richness of the luxuriously embroidered clothes may be explained by Tadmur being a centre for the manufacture of textiles. Priests wore a belted tunic and a square, flat cap mortarboard sometimes adorned by a medallion called the

---

73. Cussini, 1995, 246.
74. Will, 1992, 107, 109.
75. Parlasca, 1995, 67.

'crown of Bêl'. Their headdress differed from the conical hats worn by priests elsewhere, but resembled that of Phoenician priests and imitated those of Seleucid governors and Roman emperors. In contrast to priests in other parts of the Near East, they did not grow beards and had their hair shaved off[76]. They wore a ring on the little finger and were sometimes barefoot. For the sacrificial rites they wore local dress, but otherwise Greek or Parthian clothes.

---

76. Kaizer, 2002, 236.

CHAPTER IX

Palmyran Art

Palmyran art, characteristic of a zone from Mesopotamia through Dura-Europos to the Syrian Hawran, possesses many features peculiar to Tadmur. It emphasised florid wealth of detail and vivid colouring. Its tomb paintings at the end of the second century were spectacularly grand. Like its queen, Zenobia, gorgeously dressed and brilliantly made up, Palmyra was one of the most sumptuously decorated cities in the ancient world[1].

Its sculpture – funerary, religious and civic – is mainly characterised by the use of the frontal position, each figure being separated from its neighbours, all figures being on the same level and facing the spectator. Low reliefs which accord with frontality dominate, while round figures are rare. Palmyran art was the forerunner of Byzantine art[2]. The pose is stiff and rigid, suffused by an unearthly calm. No violent action or emotion is represented, gestures are limited, eyes are enlarged and predominantly almond-shaped. Each figure is depicted individually, with expressionless features. This art is static, not dramatic like

---

1.   Browning, 1979, 40 and 80.
2.   Millar, 1996, 329.

Hellenistic art[3]. In fact, because of its lack of movement and stylisation, it was the opposite of Graeco-Roman art. Its emphasis on detail, particularly in the depiction of jewellery and costume, indicates the social importance of this art whose objective was to represent Palmyrans as they wished to be seen[4]. Sculpture, both funerary and religious, is immediately recognisable from the frozen aspect of portraiture, eyes opened for eternity[5].

Palmyran art was original. It remained Syrian and Oriental in spite of the double influence of Hellenistic (Fig. 56) and Parthian art. The link with Parthian art goes back to the second half of the second century BC when Palmyra was in the Parthian sphere of influence, and, although Parthian art had a different vision from that of Greek art, it was in fact Graeco-Oriental (Fig. 57)[6]. It was influenced by Seleucia on the Tigris and other cities of Seleucid Mesopotamia, where Hellenistic art had developed with a strong Parthian influence. Palmyra was in contact with these centres through caravaneers and shipowners who established trading posts in those places[7].

Reliefs and funerary sculptures were the most important form of artistic expression, but most of those from tower-tombs have been pillaged and destroyed. Busts and reliefs still intact in the subterranean tombs and complexes fell

3.   Al-Bounni and al-Asa'd, 1987, 33 and 37–40.
4.   Al-As'ad and Yon, 2001, 24.
5.   Starcky, 1960, 1092.
6.   Will, 1992, 118–20.
7.   Al-Bounni and al-As'ad, 1997, 32.

prey to tomb robbers who had found a lucrative business, for the sculptures appeared on the antique market as early as in the third quarter of the nineteenth century[8].

A choice of funerary busts was available in workshops producing mortuary art (Figs. 58 and 59). Some were made while the subject was still alive, others were chiselled after death and the date inscribed according to the Seleucid era. On some, the age of the deceased was mentioned, accompanied very often by the exclamation *HBL* ('alas!'). Many shared a common formula: 'This *naphša* is that of ....', *naphša* (the term for soul) meaning here a stele or a bust. Two palm branches were depicted as a sign of victory over death, and a shroud or veil symbolised the separation of the deceased (generally in front of the veil) from the living. On some funerary reliefs, the male deceased is accompanied by a sister or a wife, who is represented weeping and with her hand touching the deceased in a gesture of consolation. On others, a mother is depicted with one or several children distinguished from the adults by their small size (since they were sculptured as men with small bodies), and frequently holding a cluster of grapes or a bird in their hands[9]. On a few beautiful and majestic sarcophagi a funerary banquet is represented in relief. Attributed to the Roman period, the earliest datable sarcophagi are older than the bulk of those from Italy[10]. On some are depicted scenes from the life of the tomb owner on

---

8. Parlasca, 1995, 59, 63, 66 and 67.
9. Al-Bounni and al-As'ad, 1987, 39.
10. Parlasca, 1995, 68.

the sidepanels, whilst on the lid, the deceased leans on one elbow, with his wife at his feet and his children behind. These sarcophagi were manufactured in Palmyra, but have also been found in Dura-Europos and Hatra. The facade of some tower tombs included a balcony with a banquet scene in relief, which, according to some scholars, depicted a banquet in the hereafter[11].

Religious statues were set along the back walls of ritual banquet chambers, sometimes within niches, and were probably votive offerings. Altars were frequently presented as offerings. The sculptured divinities were often armed and in military, local or Roman costume.

Civic statues, portraying officers, officials, senators and caravan chiefs on the brackets of the columns of the main street and in the *agora*, displayed the same frontal pose as on religious and funerary sculptures, and were Oriental in composition and style. Sculpture became more natural in the second century under the influence of Rome, and in the third century was infused with a discreet grace, partly because the material used – limestone – is less 'cold' than marble. J. Ingholt has divided Palmyran sculpture into three phases. Up to AD 150, eyes were represented by two concentric circles. Men were portrayed as beardless, women with a curl of hair on each shoulder and holding a distaff or spindle. Between AD 150 and 200, the pupils of the eyes were shown as a circle with a central dot. Women wore two or three pendants, and their hands held a garment, veil or tunic. The period AD 200–72 was characterised by growing

---

11. Al-Bounni and al-As'ad, 1987, 39.

naturalism, head turned to the side, less severe eyes and a superabundance of jewels[12].

From Parthia Palmyra took sculpture, and from Rome urbanism and architecture. Imperial civic architecture was a statement of Roman power. Graeco-Roman models were adopted in the beginning of the second century, but the break with more ancient models was not total. The tombs in their architectural forms and decoration were inspired by contemporary Graeco-Roman models, and so were the temples, such as the temples of Ba'alšamîn and Nebu, although the cults were Syrian[13]. The elaboration at Palmyra of original decorative motifs bespeaks of the existence of construction workshops of a high standard. Amongst Syrian Roman towns, Palmyra was a desert city of middling importance on the margin of mainstream artistic development[14]. Yet, grandiose Roman monuments, especially the temple of Bêl, have survived practically intact and dominate the town today.

Palmyran sculptures and reliefs are powerful, and their directness is startling, forcing the onlooker to associate the funerary reliefs with the veiled mystery of the afterlife. Their impact on the viewer is astonishing. Although the sculptures do not possess the beauty of form and harmony of Classical sculpture, they shine with a crude strength as they gaze at you, the onlooker, with their empty eyes. They look beyond

---

12. Al-Bounni and al-Asʿad, 1987, 41–3, quote Ingholt's 1935 and 1936 study of Palmyrene sculpture.
13. Al-As'ad and Yon, 2001, 127.
14. Will, 1995, 35.

you and compel you to confront the hereafter. The unearthly stillness and the absence of movement are points of no return. Forever in their House of Eternity, they force you to reflect on the nothingness that is the fate of the carnal body, and to hope for the survival of the soul beyond.

CHAPTER X

Tadmur after Zenobia

Much as the ancient sources speak of the two destructions of Palmyra by Aurelian, excavations show that the town does not bear measure of massive destruction. Aurelian's soldiers did not destroy the city completely, and it survived the first and second pillages. The temple of Bêl, the most important monument in the town, suffered damage by the III Legio Cyrenaica in revenge for Zenobia's destruction of the legion's temple of Jupiter when she swept through Bostra, the capital of the Province of Arabia, on her way to conquer Egypt. After the fall of Palmyra, the legion had a right of compensation, especially as it had remained loyal to the emperor. Aurelian, after allowing the legion to destroy parts of the temple, ordered its restoration with the money he had taken from Zenobia's treasury and from the confiscated property of the Palmyrans, respectively 300 and 1,800 pounds of gold. He even asked the Senate of Rome to send a priest to reopen the temple[1]. The administration of the temple was not affected after the conquest, thanks to the political attitude of

---

1.   Zos., *Hist. Nov.*, 1, 61; *Hist. Aug., Aurel.*, 3, 15; 'Alī, 1968–73, 125.

Fig. 46   The Valley of Tombs (Photo Studio Zouhabi, Palmyra)

Fig. 47   The tower-tomb of Jamblichus in the Valley of Tombs (Photo Studio Zouhabi, Palmyra)

Fig. 48   Hard limestone closing slab of a *loculus* (h 49 cm; w 52 cm) depicting the deceased, ca AD 200, Palmyra Museum (Courtesy of the General Directorate of Antiquities and Museums of the Syrian Arab Republic)

Fig. 49   Central corridor of the Tomb of Yarhibôl (Photo Studio Zouhabi, Palmyra)

Fig. 50 Entrance facade of the tower-tomb of Jamblichus (Photo Studio Zouhabi, Palmyra)

Fig. 51 Tower-tomb of Elahbêl (Photo Studio Zouhabi, Palmyra)

Fig. 52 Interior of the tower-tomb of Elahbêl (Photo Studio Zouhabi, Palmyra)

Fig. 53   Interior of the *hypogeum* of the Three Brothers (Photo Studio Zouhabi, Palmyra)

Fig. 54   *Hypogeum* of the Three Brothers: painted frescoes in the barrel vault (Photo Studio Zouhabi, Palmyra)

Fig. 55   Limestone statue of a warrior wearing a cuirass (h 120 cm; w 62 cm), first century AD, Palmyra Museum (Courtesy of the General Directorate of Antiquities and Museums of the Syrian Arab Republic)

Fig. 56 Hard limestone bust of a bearded man (h 38 cm; d 25 cm), second to third century AD, Palmyra Museum (Courtesy of the General Directorate of Antiquities and Museums of the Syrian Arab Republic)

Fig. 57 Hard limestone bust of priest (h 35 cm; w 18 cm), perhaps second half of second century AD, Palmyra Museum (Courtesy of the General Directorate of Antiquities and Museums of the Syrian Arab Republic)

Fig. 58 Florid vine design on a limestone low-relief carving (Photo Julien Cherlopin

Fig. 59 Amphora flanked by winged sphinxes: a syncretist design borrowing from Hellenistic, Egyptian and Parthian art (Photo Julien Charlopin)

Fig. 60 From the *agora* of Palmyra looking towards the Mamluk castle (Photo Julien Charlopin)

Haddûdân the Symposiarch who had led the capitulation party. It is indicated by an inscription erected one year after the catastrophe by the temple *thiase* in which the priests of Bêl appointed their sons to replace them in their temple functions[2].

It is probable that Aurelian assimilated Bêl with Sol Invictus whom he worshipped and regarded as the supreme god of the empire, although Bêl did not have a solar character, as did only Yarhibôl, one of his companions[3]. On his return to Rome, Aurelian built a temple which followed the Syrian rites on Quirinal Hill and consecrated it in 274 in memory of his victory. The cult of Sol Invictus (the Invincible Sun) was widespread in the Oriental provinces and in the Roman army. The temple was erected not only for Aurelian's personal devotion, but for that of various peoples of the empire. It incorporated the most beautiful section of the temple of Bêl, with accessories and jewel-encrusted robes, which Aurelian had carried from Palmyra to Rome[4]. The temple had received fifteen thousand pounds of gold and glittered with offerings[5].

The spoils which Aurelian had brought from Palmyra – horses, arms, camels, gold, silver and precious stones – were consecrated to the other gods of Rome. In Palmyra, commercial activity suffered heavily, for people no longer had the strength to keep up the line of communication from

---

2. Gawlikowski, 1971, 412, 418 and 421.
3. Starcky and Gawlikowski, 1985, 67.
4. Mommsen, 1985, 808; Scarre, 1995, 187.
5. Gibbon, 1934, 271; Hitti, 1951, 440.

Palmyra to the Gulf, the population was old, the young elite had been killed, and what was left of the merchant aristocracy could not resume its commercial activity because of the presence of the Roman garrison which exercised Roman control and made the caravans avoid the town[6].

Palmyra, defeated, depleted and partially destroyed, retained its pride and national spirit, for anti-Roman feeling ran extremely high. The nationalists conspired for revolt and came to the conclusion that in order to succeed they had to placate the official Roman authority and come to terms with its representatives in the Orient. They tried to involve Marcellinus, the prefect and governor of Mesopotamia, whom Aurelian had left behind to control the East. In an effort to neutralise him, they offered to declare him emperor. Playing for time, the prefect proposed to examine the question and postponed his answer. Meanwhile, he sent word to Aurelian informing him of the conspiracy. The national party and the local aristocracy led by Septimius Aspsaeu realised that Marcellinius had tricked them, and decided to declare the revolt immediately by proclaiming Augustus a distant relative of Odainat and Zenobia named Antiochus (a common name in Zenobia's family). They gave him the purple cloak and placed him at the head of the rebellion. Some historians claim that he was a son of Zenobia who had not been deported to Rome[7]. The rising was violent. All the inhabitants participated in the revolt,

---

6.   Kotula, 1997, 141.
7.   Zos., *Hist. Nov.*, 1, 60–1; Février, 1931, 137–8.

and the garrison which Aurelian had left in Palmyra was massacred.

The revolt in Palmyra coincided with a simultaneous revolt in Egypt. The partisans of Palmyra who had fomented the revolt in Egypt were mainly Alexandrian merchants who had suffered tremendous losses from the interruption of their commercial contacts with Palmyra, for their trade with Asia had nearly collapsed. They longed for Palmyran rule, for it had eliminated their exploitation by Rome. Besides, the commercial policy of Palmyra had suited them. On the reconquest of Egypt by the future Roman Emperor Probus, the commercial relations with the Orient had ceased for a year and there was great discontent. It was therefore natural that the merchants of Alexandria should have taken the initiative in the rebellion, encouraged by the revolt in Palmyra and the presence of Palmyran troops in Egypt which had not been destroyed by Probus in his rush together with his army, to aid Aurelian in his war against the Palmyrans. Probus had been too late to take part in the battle of Emesa, but arrived in time for the siege of Palmyra. Meanwhile, Palmyran troops in Egypt retreated to Upper Egypt and held the region[8]. Firmus, a rich Greek merchant from Seleucia who monopolised the trade in papyrus rolls and glue, and former friend and ally of Odainat and Zenobia, headed the revolt. As an importer and exporter who owned ships which sailed to India through the Red Sea and the Persian Gulf, he had contacts all over the Orient. He

---

8.   Février, 1931, 139.

also had the support of the Arabs and of the Blemmyes, who were scattered on both sides of the Red Sea. The intense resentment of Egyptians towards Roman reoccupation, which entailed a material and moral loss, made it easy for Firmus to occupy the Delta and enter Alexandria, where he immediately recognised the authority of Antiochus Augustus of Palmyra, and took the title of *Corrector* and *Imperator* – titles which had been borne by Odainat[9].

One of his first acts was to interrupt the wheat delivery to Rome. Meanwhile, he coined money, published edicts and raised an army[10]. In fact, he was obliged by the Alexandrians to defend what was left of the empire of Palmyra[11]. On learning of the turn of events, and that he had lost Syria and Egypt for the second time, Aurelian rushed back to crush both revolts. His fury must have led to the astonishing rapidity of his movement. It took him just two months to march with his army from Moesia to Palmyra, for he planned to crush Palmyra first. The inhabitants of Antioch, who had been watching a chariot race, were surprised to see the emperor approaching. The Palmyrans were shocked, for they did not expect to see him back. Palmyra was taken without resistance and delivered to pillage. As to the pretender-emperor Antiochus, he was so insignificant that Aurelian released him[12].

---

9.   Cisek, 1994, 115.
10. Gibbon, 1934, 268.
11. Schwartz, 1976, 149.
12. Zos., *Hist. Nov.,* 1, 61; *Hist. Aug. Aurel.,* 31, 3–4.

After crushing the uprising, he proceeded to Egypt where he defeated Firmus whose allies, the Blemmyes, did not arrive in time to help him. Defeated and dejected, Firmus hanged himself. Aurelian treated Alexandria savagely by razing to the ground the city walls and the rich quarter of the merchants. He also levied a new tax on all artisan products in Egypt[13]. Thus, Aurelian repossessed the Orient, and, before returning to Rome, he left two legions, one in Syria and the other in Arabia, to control the country lately occupied by the Palmyrans[14].

The savage second destruction and pillage of Palmyran monuments, walls, towers and tombs continued after Aurelian had left, and reached such a point that the emperor wrote to the commander to stop the pillage and pardon the remaining Palmyrans. The elite of the population left the town, and the caravans were directed to Bostra and Aleppo. Yet, recent excavations in the colonnaded street which survived until the 'Ayyubid period have shown that only seven years after the second destruction, Palmyrans were restoring monuments – a sign of unexpected resilience. These excavations have uncovered a mediaeval Arab market built between the columns of the main avenue, as three parallel groups of shops and narrow alleys. These shops were built of reused columns. Ten inscriptions in Palmyran and Greek were found on the bases of statues in honour of Palmyran citizens who had helped restore the once-

---

13. *Hist. Aug., Tyr. Trig.*, 5, 1–2; Kotula, 1997, 144.
14. *Hist. Aug., Aurel.*, 28, 4; Homo, 1904, 111; Cisek, 1994, 116–7.

flourishing city. These inscriptions had been carved on behalf of the tribe of Bene Mattabôl, one of the four tribes on which the government of Palmyra had rested. Each of these tribes had its own sanctuary, the temple of Arsu being the shrine of the Bene Mattabôl. One inscription, which bears the astonishing date of AD 279–80, indicates that only seven years after the destruction of the temple of Arṣu, it was repaired by Malik b. Mukumu, who with his father, had its ceiling rebuilt. This was carried out during the reign of Emperor Probus, the former general who had reconquered Egypt for Aurelian. This inscription proves that the Palmyrans kept their cults and their ancient custom of restoring monuments. The tribe of Bene Mattabôl who had honoured and raised statues to its members in AD 197, 201 and 208, as indicated by inscriptions, continued to do so in AD 279–80 after the disaster.

The shops in the vicinity of the temple were consecrated by the Bene Mattabôl to Arsu, and rents were used for the benefit of the temple, as was customary in Palmya. That this continued after 273 indicates economic continuity. The temple was finally destroyed at the end of the third century by Diocletian who used its masonry to repair Zenobia's wall[15].

With the second destruction, caravans came to an end, and Palmyra the caravan city became an important garrison town under Diocletian. In 297–8, Galerius Caesar gained a decisive victory over the Persians. The treaty of Nisibis

---

15. Al-As'ad and Gawlikowski, 1986–87, 11–15.

which followed was favourable to the Romans and lasted for forty years. The Romans kept a reserve army in Mesopotamia, and accordingly Palmyra regained its military importance as a strategic point and as a centre of a network of roads and small forts which constituted the eastern Syrian *limes*. This explains the establishment of a camp by Diocletian who had a passion for building. This sumptuous camp in the north-western part of Palmyra, raised between AD 293 and 303 under the auspices of Sussianus Hierocles, abundantly reused masonry, particularly from the Western Necropolis. The camp enclosed by a wall included the sanctuary of Allât, a military goddess identified with Athena, who was worshipped until the fourth century. Other Palmyran installations incorporated in the camp were a porticoed street of the second century and another street from the first century. A gate with three bays opened onto the forum and from there a stairway led to the *praetorium*, seat of the legion's commander. The camp was believed to have been constructed on the site of Zenobia's palace, as some reused stones date to that period, but excavations have proven otherwise[16]. With the construction of the camp thirty years after the destruction of Palmyra, Diocletian created a new town (although a large portion of the old town was maintained) which became a stronghold in the Roman *limes*[17].

---

16. Al-Bounni and al-As'ad, 1987, 90; Gawlikowski, 1995, 6.
17. Will, 1992, 197.

The policing of the desert, which for centuries had been Palmyra's prerogative, was handed over by Diocletian to 'Imru' al-Ḳays, son of 'Umar b. 'Adī of the Tanūkh, king of Ḥīra, Zenobia's traditional enemy. The inscriptions of Namara and Der'a indicate that the Arabs of Ḥīra took over the defence of the towns of the Province of Arabia after the fall of Palmyra. The inscription of Namara, written in the Arabic language but in Nabatean script, and believed to be the ancestor of the Arabic script, is actually the epitaph of 'Imru' al-Ḳays 'king of all the Arabs', and demonstrates that the Tanūkh not only assumed the role of Palmyra, but enlarged the original territory to include northern Arabia. Namara lies north-east of Djabal Duruz and was the site of a Roman fort. The inscriptions of Der'a as well as Bostra emphasise the need for strong fortifications after the fall of Palmyra[18]. Rome, however, was responsible for the defence of the frontier and Diocletian initiated the building of forts, Ḳasr al-Ḥayr and Ḳasr al-Ḥallabat, whilst his ally 'Imru' al-Ḳays began the construction of Ḳasr al-Mshattā[19] in order to fill the military and commercial vacuum produced by the destitution of Palmyra, since it had controlled the desert frontier with its turbulences and patterns of transhumance[20]. Excavations at Ḳasr al-Ḥayr, however, have established that it was built by the Umayyad Caliph Hishām b. 'Abd al–Malik in AD 728. It was a caravan resting place (a *khan*) on the route between Bostra and Aleppo. However, Palmyran

---

18. Bowersock, 1983, 134, 136 and 140; Sartre, 2001, 783 and 789.
19. Dussaud, 1955, 80–1.
20. Shahîd, 1984a, 22–3.

capitals, decorative elements and ancient Greek inscriptions indicate that a Palmyran fort had preceded the work of Hishām[21]. It is probable that Diocletian repaired a Palmyran fort which was later rebuilt by the Umayyads.

Constantine (307–37) imposed Christianity on the empire after he had defeated Licinius. In 324, pagan sacrifices were prohibited and the treasures of the pagan temples were seized. With part of this treasure, churches were built in Jerusalem and Bethlehem, but Constantine did not immediately suppress the cults of the ancient gods. The image of the solar deity is depicted on his coins till 320, for, like Aurelian and other soldier emperors, Constantine was a devotee of the sun. In 325 he summoned the Council of Nicaea, but he continued to bear the title of *Pontifex Maximus*, and was only baptised on his deathbed in 327. In Palmyra, an inscription in Greek shows that restoration work continued: an inscription dated AD 328 indicates that the curator of the town, Flavius Diogenes, restored eight bays of a portico[22]. The *cella* of Bêl became a church in the fourth century and a mosque in the twelfth century. Two new churches were built from reused materials. Pagan cults were finally abolished in Palmyra in 380 under Theodosius I (379–95). In 391, he declared Christianity to be the only official religion of the empire and prohibited pagan cults, thus resulting in the closure of temples. Palmyra became an advance post in the desert, and an episcopal see. In 325, Bishop Mainus participated in the Council of Nicaea.

---

21. Al-Bounni and al-As'ad, 1987, 122–4.
22. Février, 1931, 144; Gawlikowski, 1997, 209.

At the end of the fifth century, the Arab dynasty of the Ghassānids, who now dominated the Syrian desert and were allies of the Byzantines, used Palmyra as one of their residences[23]. In the sixth century, Emperor Justinian ordered the restoration of the town and requested Patricius the Armenian, dux of Antioch, to repair Diocletian's camp and fortify the walls[24] which encompassed the northern section of the city. He also re-established irrigation of the fields by means of a canal. During this period Palmyra was part of the inner *limes*. Arab tribes, loyal to the Romans, nomadised in the zones between the inner and outer *limes*[25].

Diocletian's camp remained in use until shortly before the Arab occupation of Palmyra in AD 634 when it opened its doors to Abū Bakr's general, Khalīd b. al-Walid. During the Umayyad eighth century, Palmyra regained some importance, being located between Ḳasr al-Ḥayr al-Gharbī (west) and Ḳasr al-Ḥayr al-Sharkī (east), both residences of the Caliph Hishām b. 'Abd al-Malik. Marwān II, the last Umayyad caliph, put down a revolt in the city and dismantled the ancient walls and Justinianic ramparts[26].

During the Umayyad period, the fourth and sixth-century-old churches were still in use. However, a new church was built in the early eighth century, the first church of this date ever found in Syria, but it was abandoned in the ninth century. The last known Bishop of Palmyra is attested in AD 818.

---

23. Al-Bounni and al-As'ad, 1987, 30–1.
24. Février, 1931, 145.
25. 'Alī, 1968–73, 129.
26. Al-Bounni and al-As'ad, 1987, 31.

Two religious communities, the Christians and Muslims, lived side by side during the Umayyad period, but the absolute end of occupation of the ancient site of Palmyra coincided with the disappearance in the ninth century of the Christian community which had lived with the Muslims within the limits of Roman Palmyra[27].

Many civic, religious and funerary sculptures were destroyed in Palmyra during the Umayyad period under the caliphate of Yazīd II (720-724) who issued a decree ordering the destruction of all human depictions in Muslims lands.

The 'Abbassīds neglected Palmyra. Recent excavations in a second-century residential quarter show that it remained inhabited until the ninth century, the time of its final abandonment[28].

Palmyra regained some importance under the Bourids of Damascus in the twelfth century, the 'Ayyūbids in the twelfth and thirteenth centuries, and the Mamlūks between the thirteenth and fifteenth centuries. The temple of Bêl was transformed into a fortress, its *cella* becoming a mosque. Other mosques, olive presses and pottery kilns were discovered dating to these periods. The castle overlooking the city which had been attributed to Ma'ān Fakhr al-din (1595–1634), probably dates to the Mamlūk period (Fig. 60).

In 1401, Tamerlane pillaged Palmyra, and during the Ottoman period (1516–1919), the city declined and was

---

27. Gawlikowski, 1997, 209 and 211.
28. Gawlikowski, 1995, 7.

reduced to a small village confined to a courtyard of the temple of Bêl, its colonnade in ruins. The French Mandatory Government evacuated the villagers from the temple and relocated them in 1929–32 in a modern village. In 1984 this numbered 30,000 inhabitants; 60,000 today. It has drinking water and a sewage system, schools and farms. Its annual revenue derives from agriculture (wheat, barley and olives) and the mining of phosphate deposits. It has roads, hotels and a museum. It attracts scholars and tourists from all over the world, and has a highly developed tourist trade. Zenobia's Tadmur has become a city again, with prospects for the future[29].

---

29. Al-Bounni and al-As'ad, 1987, 133–4.

BIBLIOGRAPHY

Ancient Classical Sources

AMMIANUS MARCELLINUS *Rerum gestarum* 28, ed. J.C.ROLFE, The Loeb Classical Library, London-Harvard, 1939, Vol. III; ed. M.-A. Marie, *Ammien Marcellin. Histoire,* Les Belles Lettres, Paris, 1984, T. V *(Livres XXVI-XXVIII).*

ARNAUD-LINDET, M.-P., *Festus. Abrégé des hauts Faits du peuple romain,* Les Belles Lettres, Paris, 1994.

PSEUDO-AURELIUS VICTOR *De Vita et Moribus Imperatorum* 35, 1-2; éd. M.FESTY, *PseudoAurelius Victor, Abrege des Cesars,* Les Belles Lettres, Paris, 1999.

EUSEBIUS CAESARENSIS *Historia Ecclesiastica,* éd. G. BARDY, *Eusebe, Histoire ecclesiastique,* Vols I-Ill, SC 31, 41, 55, Paris, 1952-1958; transl. G.A.WILLIAMSON, *History of the Church,* London, 1989, 30-78.

EUTROPIUS Breviarum Historiae Romanae 9, 13, ed. H.W. BIRD, *The Breviarum Ab Urbe Condita of Eutropius,* Liverpool University Press, Liverpool, 1993; éd. J. HELLEGOUARC'H, *Eutrope. Abrégé d'histoire romaine* I, Les Belles Lettres, Paris, 1999.

FESTUS *Sextus Pompeius Breviarum rerum gestarum populi romani* 23, 1-2; 24, 1, ed. J.W.EADIE, *The Breviarum of Festus, A Critical Edition with Historical Commentary,* London, 1967; éd.

GOULET, R. and J. PÉPIN, *Vie de Plotin,* Vols 1-11, Vrin, Paris, 1982-1992.

Historia Augusta Valeriani Duo: Les Deux Valeriens, 4, 2-4, ed. F. PASCHOUD, Les Belles Lettres, Paris, 1996a.

> *Gallieni Duo: Les deux Galliens,* 1, 1; 3,1-5; 5, 6; 10, 1-8; 12, 1-6; 13, 1-5; 16, 1-4; 19,6-7; 21, 2-5, eds O. DESBORDES and S. RATTI, Les Belles Lettres, Paris, 2001.

> *Tyranni Triginta: Les Trente Tyrans: Hérodes, Maeonius, Odenath, Zénobie,* éd. A. CHASTAGNOL, R. Laffont, Paris, 1994.

> *Divus Claudius: Le divin Claude,* 4, 4; 7, 5; 11, 1, ed. A. CHASTAGNOL, R. Laffont, Paris, 1994.

> *Divus Aurelianus: Le divin Aurélien,* 22-38, éd. F. PASCHOUD, Les Belles Lettres, Paris, 1996b.

The Scriptores Historiae Augustae, ed. D. MAGIE, The Loeb Classical Library, Vols I-Il, LondonNew York, 1922-1932: *The Two Valerians* (by Trebellius Pollio) 4, 2-4.

The Two Gallieni (by Trebellius Pollio) 1, 1; 3,1-5; 5,6; 10, 1-8; 12, 1-6; 13, 1-5; 16, 1-4; 19, 6-7); 21, 2 -5.

The Thirty Pretenders (by Trebellius Pollio).

The Deified Claudius 4,4; 7, 5; 11, 1

The Deified Aurelian (by Flavius Vopiscus of Syracuse), 22-38.

MALALAS *Chronicon* XII. 297-300,12,25; XII. 95-96,12; XII. 300b, 57; XII. 300, 8-11, 79, ed. L. DINDORF, *Malalas, Chronographia,* Corpus Scriptorum Historiae Byzantinae, Bonnae, 1831; Byzantina Australiensa 4, Melbourne, 1986.

OROSIUS *Adversus paganos* VII, 22, 10; 23, 4., Engl. transl. R.J. DEFERRARI, *The Seven Books against the Pagans,* Washington, 1964; éd. M.-P. ARNAUD-LINDET, *Orose. Histoires (Contre les Païens),* T. III, Les Belles Lettres, Paris, 1991.

PLOTINUS *Enneades* I, 4 ("Happiness"); I, 6 ("Beauty"); 11, 3 ("Are the Stars Causes?"); III, 2 ("Providence: First Treatise"); VI, 7 ("How The Multiplicity of the Ideal-Fonns Came into Being; and on the Good"), éd. G. Brehier, *Plotin, Ennéades,* Vols I-VII, Les Belles Lettres, Paris, 1924-1939; ed. A.H. Armstrong, *Plotinus, Enneads,* The Loeb Classical Library, Cambridge, Mass.-London, 1966-, Vols I-V; transl. S. MacKENNA, abridged with an introduction and notes by J. DILLON, Penguin Books, London, 1991.

PORPHYRIUS GAZAE *Vita Plotini,* ed. A.H. ARMSTRONG, *On the Life of Plotinus and the order of Plotinus and the Arrangement of his Work,* transl. S. MacKENNA, in *Plotinus The Enneads,* Penguin Books, Hannondsworth, 1991, cii-cxxv; éds L. BRISSON, M.-O. GOULET-CAZÉ,

Res Gestae divi Sapori, ed. A. MARICQ, "Classica et Orientalia", *Syria* 35 (1958), 295-360.

ZONARAS *Annales* 1, 12, ed. M. PINDER, T.I-II, in Corpus Scriptorum Historiae Byzantinae 47-48, Bonnae, 1841-1844.

ZOSIMUS *Historia Nova,* 1, 39-44 and 50-61, Engl. transl. J. BUCHANAN and H.T. DAVIS, San Antonio, Texas, 1967; ed. F. PASCHOUD, *Zosime. Histoire Nouvelle,* T. I (Livres I et II), Les Belles Lettres, Paris, 1971.

Ancient Arabic Sources (in Arabic)

AL-BAKRI   *al-Masālik w-al-Mamālik,* Algiers, 1857.

AL-DĪNAWARI   *al-Akhbār al-Tiwāl,* Cairo, 1959; 2nd ed. Baghdad.

AL-HAMADHANĪ   *Kitāb al-Buldān,* Leiden, 1902.

AL-IṢFAHANĪ   *Kitāb al-Aghānī,* Vol. 15, Dar Al-Tagafa Publications, Beirut, 1958.

AL-ḴAZWĪNĪ   *Āthār al-Bilād wa Akhbār al-'Ibād,* Vol. 15, Dar Sader Publications, Beirut, 1973.

AL-MA'SUDĪ   *Murudj al-Dhahab wa-ma'ādin al-jauhar.* Vol. 2 *al-Mutba' al-Asrya,* Baghdad, n.d.

AL-TABARĪ   *Ta'rīkh al-Rusul wa 'l-Mulūk,* Vols 1-2, Istikama Publications, Cairo, 1939.

AL-YA'ḴŪBĪ   *al-Kāmilfi 'l-Ta'rīkh,* Vol. 1, Dar Sader Publications, Beirut, 1960.

IBN AL-ATHĪR   *al-Kāmilfi 'l-Ta'rīkh,* Dar Sader Publications, Vol. 1, Beirut, 1965.

IBN AL-FAḴĪH   *Kitāb al-Buldān,* Leiden-Beirut, 1922.

IBN ḤAZM AL-ANDALUSI *Jamharat Insab al-arab,* Dar al-Ma'arīf Publications, Cairo, 1962.

IBN KHALDŪN   *Ta'rīkh,* Vol. 2, al-Ahlī Publications, Beirut, 1969.

IBN ḴUTAIBA   *Kitāb al-Shi'r,* Dar al-Ma'arīf Publications, Cairo, 1966.

YĀḴŪT   *Mujam al-Buldān,* Vol. 2, Dar al kitāb al-arabi Publications, Beirut, 1957.

Modern Sources

'ALĪ, J. (1968-1973.) *al-Mufassal fi ta'rīkh al-'arab abl al-islām,* Vol. 3, Bagdad, 1968-1973 (in Arabic).

AMY, R. (1976) "Remarques sur la construction du temple de Bel", in *Colloque Palmyre,* 53-68. *L'Arabie preislamique et son environnement historique et culturel, Actes du Colloque de Strasbourg,* 24-27 juin 1987, éd. T. FAHD, Leiden, 1989.

AS'AD, KH. AL- and GAWLIKOWSKI, M. (1986-1987) "New Honorific Inscriptions in the Great Colonnade of Palmyra", *AAS* 36-37 (1986-1987), 164-171.

AS'AD, KH. AL- and GAWLIKOWSKl, M. (1997) *The Inscriptions in the Museum of Palmyra,* Warsaw and Palmyra, 1997.

AS'AD, KH. AL- and SCHMID-COLINET, A. (1993) "Rapport des missions actives it Palmyre, 1990-1991", *Syria* 70 (1993), 567-576.

AS'AD, KH. AL- and YON, J.-B. (2001) *Inscriptions de Palmyre,* Direction Générale des Antiquités et des Musées de la République Arabe Syrienne-Institut Français d'Archéologie du Proche-Orient, Beyrouth-Damas-Amman, 2001.

BAUZOU, TH. (1996) "Deux milliaires inédits de Vaballath en Jordanie du Nord", *in* PH. FREEMAN and D. KENNEDY eds, *The Defence of the Roman and Byzantine East,* BAR International Series 297(i), Oxford, 1996, 1-8.

BERCHEM, D. Van (1976) "Le plan de la ville de Palmyre", in *Colloque Palmyre,* 165-173.

BESNIER, M. (1937) "Les empereurs illyriens (268-285)", in *L'empire romain de l'avènement des Sévères au Concile de Nicée,* Histoire generale IIIᵉ partie, t. IV, Ch. 6, colI. Glotz, Paris, 1937, 225-265.

BOUNNI, A. AL- (1965) "A relief in Tadmur attributed to Al-Zaba", *AAS* 15 (1965), 1-14.

BOUNNI, A. AL- (1967) "Bilan de dix annees d'explorations à Palmyre", *Archeologia* 16 (mai-juin 1967), 40-49.

BOUNNI, A. AL- (1972) "Medieval Arabic text in Tadmur", *AAS* 22 (1972), 73-79.

BOUNNI, A. AL- (1978) *Tadmur and Tadmurites,* Damascus, 1978 (in Arabic).

BOUNNI, A. AL- (1996) "Zenobia of History and al-Zaba of legend", in *International Seminar on Tadmur and the Silk Road,* Damascus, 1996, 215-219 (in Arabic).

BOUNNI, A. AL- and AS'AD, KH. AL-.(l987) *Palmyra: History, Monuments and Museum,* Damascus, 1987; 4th ed., 2000.

Dr A. al-Bounni, History and Monuments are his Abode: Achievements of his Life. Hommage to A. al-Bounni, Ithad al-Kitāb al-Arāb, Damascus, 2002 (in Arabic).

BOWERSOCK, G.W. (1973) "Syria under Vespasian", *JRS* 63 (1973), 133-140.

BOWERSOCK, G.W. (1983) *Roman Arabia,* Harvard University Press, Cambridge, Mass, 1983.

BOWERSOCK, G.W. (1990) *Hellenism in Late Antiquity,* Cambridge-New York, 1990.

BROWNING, I. (1979) *Palmyra,* Chatto & Windus, London, 1979.
Cambridge Ancient History, Vol. XII *(The Imperial Crisis and Recovery, AD* 193-324), Cambridge, 1939, repr. 1971.

CHRISTOL, M. (1997) *L'empire romain au troisieme siecle,* Errance, Paris, 1997.

CISEK, E. (1994) *L'Empereur Aurelien et son temps,* Les Belles Lettres, Paris, 1994.

COLLEDGE, M.A.R. (1976a) "Le temple de Bel à Palmyre, qui l'a fait et pourquoi?", in *Colloque Palmyre, 45-52.*

COLLEDGE, M.A.R. (l976b) *The Art of Palmyra,* London, 1976.

CUSSINI, E. (1995) "Transfer of property at Palmyra", *Aram* 7 (1995), 233-250.

DAUPHIN, C.M. (1979) "A Roman Mosaic from Nablus", *Israel Exploration Journal* 29 (1979), 11-33.

DEGEORGE, G. (1987) *Palmyre, métropole du désert,* Paris, 1987.

DENTZER-FEYDI, J. (1993) "La mort it Palmyre", in J. DENTZER-FEYDY and J. TEIXIDOR éds, *Les antiquites de Palmyre au Musée du Louvre,* Réunion des Musées Nationaux, Paris, 1993, 57-81.

DENTZER-FEYDY, J. and J. TEIXIDOR (1993 éds), *Les antiquités de Palmyre au Musée du Louvre,* Reunion des Musées Nationaux, Paris, 1993.

DILLON, J. (1991) "Plotinus: An Introduction", in *Plotinus, The Enneads,* transl. S. MacKENNA, Penguin Books, Harmondsworth, 1991, lxxxiv-ci.

DOWNEY, G. (1950) "Aurelian's victory over Zenobia at Immae A.D. 272", *TAPA* 81 (1950), 57-68.

DOWNEY, G. (1961) *A History of Antioch in Syria from Seleucus to the Arab Conquest,* Princeton University Press, Princeton, 1961.

DRIJVERS, H.J.W. (1995) "Inscriptions from Allât's sanctuary", *Aram* 7 (1995),109-119.

DUNANT, C. (1983) "Vie et mort d'une cité: l'exemple de Palmyre", in *La ville dans le Proche-Orient ancien,* Université de Geneve, Geneve, 1983, 139-145.

DUSSAUD, R. (1927) *Topographie historique de la Syrie antique et médiévale,* Librairie Orientaliste Paul Geuthner, Paris, 1927.

DUSSAUD, R. (1957) *La pénétration des Arabes en Syrie avant l'Islam,* Bibliotheque archeologique et historique LIX, Librairie Orientaliste Paul Geuthner, Paris, 1955.

The Encyclopaedia of Islam. A Dictionary of the Geography, Ethnography and Biography of the Muhammadan Peoples, eds M. TH. HOUTSMA, T.W. ARNOLD, R. BASSET and R. HARTMANN, Vols I-IV, E.J. Brill, Leiden, 1913-1936 (Supplement, 1938).

EQUINI SCHNEIDER, E. (1993) *Septimia Zenobia Sebaste,* Studia Archaeologica 61, "l'Erma" di Bretschneider, Roma, 1993.

FÉVRIER, J.G. (1931) *Essai sur l'histoire politique et économique de Palmyre,* Vrin, Paris, 1931.

FÉVRIER, J.G. (1932) *La religion des Palmyréniens,* Vrin, Paris, 1932.

FRÉZOUL, E. (1976) "Questions d'urbanisme palmyrénien", in *Colloque Palmyre, 191-207.*

GAFFIOT, J.-CL., LAVAGNE, H. et HOFFMAN, J.-M. éds, *Moi Zenobie Reine de Palmyre,* Exposition 18 septembre – 16 decembre 2002, Centre culturel du Pantheon, Paris.

GAGÉ, J. (1964) *La montee des Sassanides,* Paris, 1964.

GAWLIKOWSKI, M. (1970) *Monuments funeraires de Palmyre,* PWN Éditions Scientifiques de Pologne,Warszawa, 1970.

GAWLIKOWSKI, M. (1971) "Inscriptions de Palmyre: Aurelien et le temple de Bel", *Syria* 48 (1971), 406-426.

GAWLIKOWSKI, M. (1974) "Les defenses de Palmyre", *Syria* 51 (1974), 231-242.

GAWLIKOWSKI, M. (1976) "Les defenses de Palmyre", in *Colloque Palmyre, 209-211.*

GAWLIKOWSKI, M. (1985a) "Les princes de Palmyre", *Syria* 62 (1985), 251-261.

GAWLIKOWSKI, M. (1985b) *Palmyre,* Paris, 1985 (updated new edition of J. Starcky, *Palmyre,* 1932).

GAWLIKOWSKI, M. (1990) "Les dieux de Palmyre", *ANRW II 18, 4* (1990), 2605-2658.

GAWLIKOWSKI, M. (1993) "Rapport des missions actives cl Palmyre 1990-1991: Palmyre, mission polonaise 1990; Palmyre, mission polonaise1991", *Syria* 70 (1993), 562-567.

GAWLIKOWSKI, M. (1995) "News from Palmyra: Current Work in Perspective", *Aram* 7 (1995), 1-7.

GIBBON, E. (1934) *The Decline and Fall ofthe Roman Empire,* New York, 1934.

GRAF, D.F. (1989a) "Rome and the Saracens: Reassessing the Nomadic Menace", in *Colloque Arabie, 341-400*.

GRAF, D.F. (1989b) "Zenobia and the Arabs", in D.H. FRENCH and C.S. LIGHTFOOT eds, *The Eastern Frontier of the Roman Empire*, BAR International Series 553(i), Oxford, 1989, 143-167.

HADAS, M. (1958) *A History of Rome from its origins to 529 AD as told by the Roman historians*, Bell, London, 1958.

ḤĀLAK, M. (2002) "Dr A. al-Bounni, a Symphony of Ṣufī love in the presence of Zenobia", in *Dr A. al-Bounni, History and Monuments are his Abode: Achievements of his Life. Hommage to A. al-Bounni*, Ithad al-Kitāb aI-Arāb, Damascus, 2002 (in Arabic).

ALLET, J. and SKINNER, M.B. (1998) *Roman Sexualities*, Princeton University Press, Princeton, 1998.

HENRY, P. (1991) "The Place of Plotinus in the History of Thought", in *Plotinus, The Enneads*, transl. S. MacKENNA, Penguin Books, Harmondsworth, 1991, xlii-lxxxiii.

HILLERS, D.R. (1995) "Notes on Palmyrene Aramaic texts", *Aram* 7 (1995), 73-88.

HITTI, P. (1951) *History of Syria*, Macmillan, London, 1951; Arabic transl. Vol. 1, Beirut, 1958.

HITTI, P. (1956) *History of the Arabs*, 5th ed., Macmillan, London, 1956; Arabic transl. Vol. 1, Beirut, 1958.

HOMO, L. (1904) *Essai sur le regne d'Aurélien*, Paris, 1904.

INOHOLT (1976) "Varia Tadmorea", in Colloque Palmyre, 101-137.

INOHOLT (1935) "Five Dated Tombs from Palmyra", Berytus 2 (1935), 57-120.

INOHOLT (1936) "Inscriptions and Sculptures from Palmyra", Berytus 3 (1936), 83-125 Inventaire des Insriptions de Palmyre, éd. J. CANTINEAU, Vols 1-9, Damas, 1930-1936; Vol. 10, éd. J. STARCKY, Damas, 1949; Vol. 11, éd. J. TEIXIDOR, Beirut, 1965; Vol. 12, eds A. AL-BOUNNI and J. TEIXIDOR, Beirut, 1976.

JONES, A.H.M. (1971) The Cities of the Eastern Roman Provinces, 2nd ed., Clarendon Press, Oxford, 1971.

KAIZER, T. (2002) The Religious Life of Palmyra. A Study of the Social Patterns of Worship in the Roman Period, Oriens et Occidens Band 4, Franz Steiner Verlag, Stuttgart, 2002.

KIYOHIDE, S. (1995) "Excavation at Southeast Necropolis in Palmyra from 1990 to 1995", Aram 7 (1995), 19-28.

KOTULA, T. (1997) Aurélien et Zénobie: l'unite ou la division de l'empire, Wydawnictwo Universitetu Wroclawskiego, 1966; transl. S. CHANTRY, Paris, 1997.

LAMMENS, H. (1928) L 'Arabie occidentale avant l'Hegire, Beirut, 1928.

LE BOHEC, Y. (1997) L 'Empire romain de la mort de Commode à Nicée, Paris, 1997.

LEVI DELLA VIDA, G. (1944) "Pre-Islamic Arabia", in The Arab Heritage, in N.A. FARIS ed., Princeton, 1944.

LORIOT, X. and NONY, D. (1997) La crise de l'Empire romain, 235-285, Armand Colin, Paris, 1997, 235-285.

MARAQTEN, M. (1995) "The Arabic words in Palmyrene inscriptions", Aram 7 (1995), 89-108.

MARE, W.H. (1995) "Abila and Palmyra: Ancient Trade and Trade Routes from Southern Syria into Mesopotamia, Aram 7 (1995), 189-215.

MATTINGLY, G. (1995) "The Palmyrene luxury trade and Revelation: a neglected analogue", Aram 7 (1995), 214-232.

MESNIL DU BUISSON, R. DU (1962) *Les Tessères et monnaies de Palmyre*, E. de Broccard, Paris, 1962.

MICHALOWSKI, K. (1967) "Lumières sur le camp de Dioclétien et la Vallée des Tombeaux à Palmyre", Archeologia 16 (mai-juin 1967), 57-63.

MILLAR, F. (1969) "P. Herennius Dexippus: the Greek World and the Third-Century Invasions", JRS 59 (1969), 12-29.

MILLAR, F. (1971) "Paul of Samosata, Zenobia and Aurelian: the Church, local culture and political allegiance in third-century Syria", JRS 61 (1971), 1-17.

MILLAR, F. (1996) The Roman Near East, 31 BC – AD 337, Harvard, 1996.

MOMMSEN, TH. (1985) "Les provinces dans l'empire", in *L'Histoire romaine*, VI, transl. A. COGNAT and J. TOULAIN, R. Laffont, Paris, 1985.

ÖNAL, M. (2002) *Mosaics of Zeugma*, A Turizm Yayinlari, Istanbul, 2002.

Palmyre, Bilan et perspectives, Colloque de Strasbourg (12-20 octobre 1973) organise par le CR.P.O.G.A. à la memoire de Daniel Schlumberger et de Henri Seyrig, Université des Sciences humaines de Strasbourg, Travaux du Centre de Recherche sur le Proche-Orient et la Grece antiques, AECR, Strasbourg, 1976.

PARLASCA, K. (1995) "Some problems of Palmyrene plastic art", Aram 7 (1995), 59-71. PEROWNE, S. (1962) Caesars and Saints: The Evolution of the Christian State 180-313 A.D., London, 1962.

PIERSIMONI, P. (1995) "Compiling a Palmyrene Prosopography: Methodological Problems", Aram 7 (1995), 251-260. Polish Archaeology in the Mediterranean, Report 1997, IX, Polish Centre of Mediterranean Archaeology, Warsaw University, Warsaw, 1998.

POTTER, D.S. (1990) Prophecy and History in the Crisis of the Roman Empire: a historical commentary on the Thirteenth Sibylline Oracle, Oxford, 1990.

REY-COQUAIS, J.-P. (1978) "Syrie romaine de Pompée à Dioclétien", JRS 68 (1978), 44-73.

SADURSKA, A. (1977) Palmyre VII. Le tombeau de la famille de Alainé, Varsovie, 1977.

SARTRE-FAURIAT, A. (1997) "Palmyre de la mort de Commode à Nicée (193-325 ap. J.-C.)", in ed. J.LE BOHEC, L'Empire romain de la mort de Commode à Nicée, Paris, 1997, 251-277.

SARTRE, M. (1982) Trois études sur l'Arabie romaine et byzantine, Latomus, Bruxelles, 1982.

SARTRE, M. (1991) L'Orient romain. Provinces et sociétés provinciales en Méditerranée orientale d'Auguste aux Sévères (31 avant J.-C. – 235 apres J.C.), Seuil, Paris, 1991.

SARTRE, M. (2001) D'Alexandre à Zénobie: histoire du Levant antique avant J.-C. IIIème s. apres J.-C., Fayard, Paris, 200l.

SCARRE, C. (1995) Chronicle of the Roman Emperors: the reign-by-reign record of the rulers of imperial Rome, London, 1995; Chronique des empereurs romains, French transl. MARUEJOT, Casterman, Paris, 1995.

SCHWARTZ, J. (1976) "Palmyre et l'opposition à Rome en Egypte", in Colloque Palmyre, 139-15l. SEYRIG, H. (1932) "L'incorporation de Palmyre à l'empire romain", Syria 12 (1932), 266-277.

SEYRIG, H. (1949) "Antiquités syriennes: notes sur Hérodien, Prince de Palmyre", Syria 26 (1949), 1-4.

SEYRIG, H. (1963) "Les fils du roi Odainat", AAS 13 (1963), 160-172.

SEYRIG, H. (1971) "Antiquités syriennes: Bel de Palmyre", Syria 48 (1971), 85-114.

SEYRIG, H. (1985) Scripta varia: mélanges d'Archéologie et d'Histoire, Librairie Orientaliste Paul Geuthner, Paris, 1985.

SHAHÎD, I. (1984a) *Rome and the Arabs. A Prolegomenon to the Study of Byzantium and the Arabs,* Dumbarton Oaks Research Library and Collection, Washington D.C., 1984.

SHAHÎD, I. (1984b) *Byzantium and the Arabs in the Fourth Century,* Dumbarton Oaks Research Library and Collection, Washington D.C., 1984.

SIRINELLI, J. (1995) *Les enfants d'Alexandrie,* Fayard, Paris, 1995.

STARCKY, J. (1960) "Palmyre", in *Supplément au Dictionnaire de la Bible,* éd. H. CAZELLES, Letouzey et Ané, Paris, 1960, T. VI, 1066-1103.

STARCKY, J. (1967) "Palmyre, metropole du desert de Syrie", *Archeologia* 16 (mai-juin 1967), 30-39.

STARCKY, J. and GAWLIKOWSKI, M. (1985) *Palmyre,* Paris, 1985 (updated repr. of J. STARCKY, *Palmyre,* Paris, 1932).

STEMBERGER, G. (1996) *Introduction to the Talmud and Midrash,* 2nd ed., T. & T. Clark, Edinburgh, 1996.

STIERLIN, H. (1987) *Cités du Désert. Pétra, Palmyre, Hatra,* Office du Livre, Fribourg, 1987.

STONEMAN, R. (1992) *Palmyra and its Empire. Zenobia's Revolt against Rome,* The University of Michigan Press, Ann Arbor, 1992.

SYME, R. (1983) *Historia Augusta Papers,* The Clarendon Press, Oxford, 1983.

AL-TAHA, A. (1982) "Men's costume in Palmyra", *AAS* 32 (1982), 17-132.

TEIXIDOR, J. (1979) "The pantheon of Palmyra", in *Etudes préliminaires aux religions orientales de l'Empire romain,* 79, Leiden, 1979, 29-34.

TEIXIDOR, J. (1981) *L'hellénisme des Barbares: l'exemple syrien. Le temps de la réflexion,* Paris, 1981.

TEIXIDOR, J. (1984) "Un port romain dans le désert: Palmyre et son commerce d'Auguste a Caracalla", *Semitica* 34 (1984), 1-125.

TEIXIDOR, J. (1993) "Ecriture et langue palmyréniennes", in J. DENTZER-FEYDY and J. TEIXIDOR eds, *Les antiquites de Palmyre au Musée du Louvre,* Réunion des Musées Nationaux, Paris, 1993, 45-50.

TEIXIDOR, J. (1997-1998) "Antiquites semitiques", *Annuaire du Collège de France, 1997-1998,* Paris, 713-736.

TRIMINGHAM, J.S. (1990) *Christianity among the Arabs in Pre-Islamic Times,* Beirut, 1990.

VAUGHAN, A.C. (1967) *Zenobia of Palmyra,* Doubleday and Co Inc., Garden City, New York, 1967.

WATSON, A. (1998) *Aurelian and the Third Century,* Routledge, London, 1998.

WILL, E. (1949) "La tour funeraire de Palmyre", *Syria* 26 (1949), 87-116.

WILL, E. (1957) "Marchands et chefs de caravane à Palmyre", *Syria* 34 (1957), 262-277.

WILL, E. (1966) "Le sac de Palmyre", in *Melanges d'archeologie et d'histoire offerts à André Piganiol,* ed. R. CHEVALLIER, S.E.V.P.E.N., Paris, 1966, 1409-1416.

WILL, E. (1983) "Le developpement urbain de Palmyre: temoignage epigraphique", *Syria* 60 (1983), 69-8l.

WILL, E. (1990) "La maison d'éternite et les conceptions funeraires des Palmyreniens", in *Melanges P. Lévêque. IV. Religion,* Annales litteraires de l'Universite de Besançon No. 413, Centre de recherché d'histoire ancienne, No. 96, 1990,433-440.

WILL, E. (1992) *Les Palmyreniens. La Venise des sables, 1er-III^{e}s.,* Armand Colin, Paris, 1992.

WILL, E. (1995) "Architecture locale et architecture imperiale à Palmyre", *Aram* 7 (1995), 29-35.

ZAHRAN, Y. (2001) *Philip the Arab. A Study in Prejudice,* Stacey International, London, 2001.

ZAYADINE, F. (1985) "Recent Excavation and Restoration at Qasr el Bint of Petra", *ADAJ* 29 (1985), 239-249.

ZENOBIA. *Il Sogno di Una Regina d'Oriente, Palazzo Bricherasio, Torino,* 13 *febbraio-26 maggio 2002,* Electa, Milano, 2002.

ZUHDI, B. (1982) "Embroidered Textiles of Tadmor", *AAS* 32 (1982), 164-166.

Index

216